はしがき

　2013年4月、政府の教育再生実行本部である成長戦略に資するグローバル人材育成部会において、「グローバルに活躍する人材を年10万人育成する」との提言がなされて以降、世界と日本の距離がますます縮まってきているのを実感します。そして、2020年の東京オリンピック開催に向けて、道路標識がローマ字表記から英語表記へと変更されたり、案内図記号および地図記号が改定されたり変更されたりしています。海外へ出て行くまでもなく、日本にいながらにして多文化や多言語に触れる機会、また、英語話者と接触し交流する機会が増える日が確実に近づきつつあります。

　異文化や異国という明確な境界線が次第に曖昧なものとなり、海外がより身近に感じられつつある今日こそ、自己を表現したり、他者を受け入れ相互理解を深化させたりする手段としての英語に真摯に向き合っていく姿勢が今まで以上に必要になるでしょう。

　このテキストは、語学学習における4技能の中で、特にリスニングとスピーキングのスキルを向上させ、音声を中心にコミュニケーションを図る活動に繋げることを目的としています。作成に当たっては、著者のアメリカやイギリス、オーストラリアなどでの生活体験、海外の大学に日本人学生を引率した体験、また、日本の大学における授業体験などから得たことをできるだけ多く取り入れ、学習者が無理なく英語学習に取り組むことができ、英語ネイティブが日常的に使うオーセンティックな英語表現を修得できるように心がけました。内容としては、神戸の大学に通う主人公アオイが、日本文化を研究するためオーストラリアから留学してきた大学院生エミリーと親しくなり、二人で台湾、香港、シンガポール、オーストラリアを旅するというプロットです。各国の有名スポットをめぐる旅と関連させた場面設定で英語学習ができるため、語学学習のみならず学習者の異文化への知的好奇心を刺激する一冊になると確信しています。

Words & Phrases
各ユニットに出てくる重要な単語やフレーズの適切な意味を、与えられたものの中から選び、学びます。

Warm-up
状況設定に応じた短いダイアログを聴いて、空所補充をする問題があります。

Exercise 1
並べかえ英作文を完成した後、音声を聴いてその英文を確認する問題があります。

Exercise 2
音声を聴いて、空所に入る最も適切な語を与えられた選択肢の中から選ぶ問題があります。

Exercise 3
音声を聴いて空所を補充する問題と、質問に対する答を与えられた選択肢の中から選ぶ問題があります。

Challenge Corner
音声を聴いて書き取る問題と、質問に対する答を与えられた選択肢の中から選ぶ問題があります。

本テキストに準備されている音声を聴きながら、英語ネイティブが日常的に使っている表現を繰り返し何度もリスニングをしたり、シャドーイングをしたり、スピーキングの練習をしたりすれば、リスニングスキルはもちろんのこと、スピーキング、リーディング、ライティングのスキルも知らず知らずのうちに確実に向上していくでしょう。特にリスニングスキルをアップさせたい学習者にとって、本テキストは必ず役に立つはずです。学習者の皆さんのゆるみない努力を期待しています。

　このテキストは学習者の英語習熟度に応じて、半期でも通年でも使用することができます。半期で使用する場合は1ユニットを1回の授業で、通年で使用する場合は小テストや復習テストなどを行いながら、半期でユニット8まで終わることを目安としてください。

　最後に、テキスト作成にあたり様々なアドバイスをしてくださった松柏社の森有紀子氏に心から御礼申し上げます。

　　2018年10月

行時　潔
今川　京子
Antony J. Parker

Contents

#	Title		Description	Page
1	Nice to Meet You! Aoi Meets Emily		初対面の人に英語で話しかける	06
2	Making Plans to Travel Together		英会話で友だちになる	10
3	Taiwan: Experiencing Traditional Culture		日常会話―観光	14
4	Taiwan: Outside Taipei		ツアーガイドとの会話―観光	18
5	Hong Kong: What a Wonderful Night View!		日常会話＋eメールで―観光	22
6	Hong Kong: Dinner on a Floating Restaurant?		日常会話＋SNSで―観光	26
7	At Hong Kong International Airport: A New Friend		到着後の空港では―初対面の人と英語で話す	30
8	Thailand: The Land of Smiles		機内では―観光	34
9	Singapore: A Multiethnic Society		ツアーガイドとの会話―観光	38
10	Singapore: High Tea at the Raffles Hotel, Anyone?		日常会話＋eメールで―観光	42
11	Perth: Emily's Family Meets Aoi		到着後の空港では	46
12	Perth: Where City Meets Outback		友だちの家族宅に泊まる―観光	50
13	Sydney: The Harbour City		日常会話―観光	54
14	Cairns: Gateway to the Reef		到着後の空港では／タクシーに乗ったら	58
15	Back in Japan		日常会話＋SNSで	62

Characters
登場人物紹介

台湾、香港、シンガポール、オーストラリアへ旅行

主人公
Aoi アオイ
神戸の大学生。ロサンゼルスの大学の語学研修に参加した経験がある。

Emily エミリー
オーストラリアのパースにある大学で比較文化を研究している大学院生。アオイが通う大学に留学中。

Jack ジャック
オーストラリアのアデレード出身。夢は大学卒業後に日本で英語を教えること。

Taiwan

Judy ジュディ
アオイがロサンゼルスの大学の語学研修に参加していた時にジュディの家にホームステイしていた。アオイは旅行中、eメールとSNSでやりとり。

Hong Kong

Singapore

アオイとエミリーは、エミリーの実家に泊まりに行く

Emily's Family

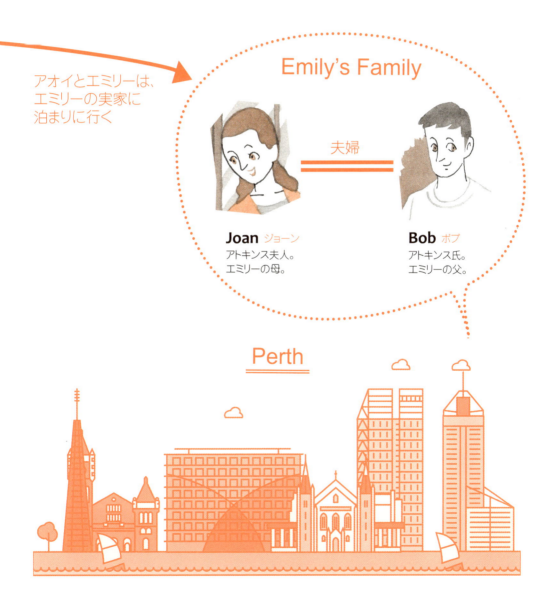

Joan ジョーン
アトキンス夫人。
エミリーの母。

夫婦

Bob ボブ
アトキンス氏。
エミリーの父。

Perth

Unit 1 Nice to Meet You! Aoi Meets Emily
初対面の人に英語で話しかける

アオイは神戸の大学に通う3回生。エミリー・アトキンスはオーストラリアのパースにある大学で比較文化を研究している大学院生。彼女はアオイが通う大学で6月の下旬から留学生として日本文化を研究している。アオイとエミリーは初対面の日から意気投合し、何でも話し合える大の仲良しになる。

Words & Phrases 次の1～10の語または語句の最も適切な意味を下のa～jから選びなさい。

1. graduate student
2. culture
3. major in
4. quite a few times
5. literature
6. fifth-grade
7. speaking of
8. according to
9. forecast
10. elementary school

- a. 文学
- b. 小学校
- c. 予報
- d. 大学院生
- e. 5年生
- f. かなり頻繁に
- g. …と言えば
- h. 文化
- i. (発言・文献・時計など)によれば
- j. …を専攻する

Warm-up 音声を聴いて、1～3のダイアログの空所を埋めましょう。

 Audio 1-02

At the university cafeteria

1. **Aoi:** Hi. Is this seat ¹_____?
   Emily: No. Please ²____ down.
   Aoi: Thank you. … I've seen you here quite a few times before.

2. **Aoi:** Where are you from, Emily?
   Emily: I'm from Perth, Australia.
   Aoi: Perth? I've never ³_____ of it. Is it ⁴_____ to Sydney?

3. **Aoi:** What are you studying at this university?
   Emily: I'm a ⁵_____ student. I'm studying Japanese culture.
   Aoi: Oh, really? I'm majoring in American ⁶_____.

Exercise 1

1〜7の（　）内の語または語句を並べかえて英文を完成させましょう。ただし、文頭にくるものも小文字で与えています。次に音声を聴いて答を確認しましょう。

🔊 Audio 1-03

1. 私は大学3年生です。
(student, a, third-year, I, university, am).
_____

2. 私は比較文化を研究している大学院生です。
I'm (student, a, studying, culture, graduate, comparative).
_____

3. 6月はオーストラリアでは冬の季節の始まりです。
(of, Australia, winter, is, the, June, in, start).
_____

4. あなたはスワン川の魅力のとりこになるでしょう。
You (enchanted, the charm, be, of, with, will) the Swan River.
_____

5. 神戸からパースまでどれくらいの距離ありますか。
(is, Kobe, far, how, to, it, from) Perth?
_____

6. 日本とパースの時差は1時間です。
(difference, Perth, between, and, Japan, the, is, time) one hour.
_____

7. 私は世界中を旅してまわることにとても興味があります。
I'm (around, in, very, world, interested, the, traveling).
_____

Exercise 2

1〜4の英文の音声を聴いて、（ ＊ ）に入る語をa〜cから選び、記号で答えなさい。

🔊 Audio 1-04

1. (　　)(　　)(＊)(　　)(　　), isn't it?
　a. is　　　b. cafeteria　　c. always

2. (　　)(　　)(＊)(　　)(　　) this university?
　a. come　　b. you　　　　c. did

3. (　　)(　　)(＊)(　　)(　　) for about five weeks.
　a. have　　b. holidays　　c. winter

4. It commences (　　)(　　)(＊)(　　)(　　).
　a. end　　　b. the　　　　c. of

初対面の人に英語で話しかける

Exercise 3　音声を聴いて、ダイアログの空所 1 ～ 4 を埋めましょう。次に 1 ～ 3 の質問に対する答として最も適切なものを a ～ c の中から選びましょう。

🔊 Audio 1-05

At the university cafeteria

Emily: This cafeteria is always crowded, isn't it?
このカフェテリアはいつも混んでるよね？

Aoi: It sure is. We are lucky to ¹(　　　)(　　　) today!
By the way, when did you come to this university?
ええ。今日は空席があってとてもラッキー！ ところで、いつこの大学に来たの？

Emily: In late June. In Australia, the first semester ends around the ²(　　　)(　　　) of June at most universities.
6月の下旬。オーストラリアではほとんどの大学の前期は6月の最終週くらいで終わるの。

Aoi: Really!?
本当！？

Emily: Yes. Then we have winter holidays for about five weeks.
そう。それから5週間ほど冬休みよ。

Aoi: Winter holidays?
冬休み？

Emily: That's right. Australia is in the Southern Hemisphere, remember?
そうなの。オーストラリアは南半球にあるのを忘れないでね。

Aoi: Of course. I forgot ³(　　　)(　　　)(　　　).
And when does the second semester commence?
そうだったわ。すっかり忘れてた。それで、後期はいつ始まるの？

Emily: It commences at the end of July and ends around the end of November. After the finals we have ⁴(　　　)(　　　)(　　　) of summer vacation.
7月の下旬に始まって、11月の下旬に終わるわ。それから定期試験があって、3か月くらい夏休みよ。

1. Where are Aoi and Emily?
   a. In the library　　b. In the classroom　　c. At the cafeteria
2. How long are the winter holidays for Australian university students?
   a. About five weeks　　b. About four weeks　　c. About three weeks
3. When does the summer vacation probably start at Australian universities?
   a. In June　　b. In August　　c. In December

Challenge Corner

ダイアログの音声を聴いて、□□□の部分を書き取り、1〜3の質問に対して最も適切な答をa〜cの中から選びましょう。

One day in December in Aoi's living room

▶▶▶▶ ◀◀◀◀   🔊 Audio 1-06

Aoi: My mother's best friend, Peggy, and her daughter from San Francisco visited us during the Christmas holidays last year.

Emily: Oh, really? Was it their first time to visit Japan?

Aoi: No. But _____ to visit us in Kobe.

1. Had Peggy and her daughter been to Kobe before?
   a. No, they hadn't.   b. Yes, they had.   c. It's not mentioned.

▶▶▶▶ ◀◀◀◀   🔊 Audio 1-07

Emily: Speaking of Christmas, I've never experienced Christmas in winter.

Aoi: According to the weather forecast, _____ around Christmas time this year.

Emily: Sounds great! How lucky I will be to have a white Christmas!

2. What will the weather be like around Christmas this year?
   a. It'll be sunny.   b. It may snow.   c. It may rain.

▶▶▶▶ ◀◀◀◀   🔊 Audio 1-08

Aoi: Have you been to Tokyo Disneyland?

Emily: No, I haven't. Have you?

Aoi: Yes, I have. My parents took me there _____ fifth grade.

3. When did Aoi go to Tokyo Disneyland?
   a. When she was an elementary school student
   b. When she was a junior high school student
   c. When she was a high school student

Unit 2 Making Plans to Travel Together
英会話で友だちになる

エミリーはクリスマスと新年を神戸で迎える。彼女は後期のテストが終わったら春休みを利用して台湾、香港、シンガポールを旅しながら、オーストラリアに一時的に帰国するので、アオイは一緒に行くことにする。アオイはアメリカ西海岸への語学留学の経験はあるが、海外旅行は今回が初めて。

Words & Phrases 次の1～10の語または語句の最も適切な意味を下のa～jから選びなさい。

1. in particular
2. while
3. apply for
4. departure
5. how about
6. this time of year
7. pack
8. tip
9. view
10. can't wait to

a. 景色　　b. 申請する　　c. ・・・はいかがですか　　d. ・・・したくてたまらない
e. 助言　　f. 出発　　　　g. 特に　　　　　　　　　　h. ・・・している間に
i. この季節　j. (持ち物をトランクなどに) 詰める

Warm-up 音声を聴いて、1～3のダイアログの空所を埋めましょう。 Audio 1-09

1. **Aoi:** What are you going to do [1]_____ the spring holidays?
   Emily: I'm [2]_____ to go back to Australia.
   Aoi: Really? Can I go with you?

2. **Emily:** I am so excited to be [3]_____ to Taiwan, Hong Kong, and Singapore.
   Aoi: So am I. I've always wanted to go to those places.
   Emily: Where in [4]_____ would you like to go in Taiwan?

3. **Emily:** Did you go to New York [5]_____ you were in Los Angeles last year?
   Aoi: No. But I went to Tijuana with my [6]_____ .
   Emily: Tijuana? That's in Mexico, right? Well, how was it?

Exercise 1
1～7の（　）内の語または語句を並べかえて英文を完成させましょう。ただし、文頭にくるものも小文字で与えています。次に音声を聴いて答を確認しましょう。

🔊 Audio 1-10

1. 私は10年有効のパスポートを持っています。
   (a, for, have, passport, ten years, I, that's, valid).
   _____

2. 海外に行く前に旅行保険に入るべきです。
   (overseas, before, you, insurance, going, should, travel, take out).
   _____

3. 彼女は台湾に行くのは今回が初めてです。
   (first, is, to, to, this, time, her, go) Taiwan.
   _____

4. 私は台湾の温泉に行ってみたいです。
   I (a, to, to, hot spring, go, in, want, Taiwan).
   _____

5. 私たちは台湾と香港では2泊ずつするつもりです。
   (two, both, we, nights, will, in, have) Taiwan and Hong Kong.
   _____

6. 彼女はシンガポールに3度行ったことがあります。
   (has, to, three, she, Singapore, times, been).
   _____

7. 私たちはパースにはシンガポール経由で行きます。
   (Singapore, to, flying, Perth, we're, via).
   _____

Exercise 2
1～4の英文の音声を聴いて、（ ＊ ）に入る語をa～cから選び、記号で答えなさい。

🔊 Audio 1-11

1. (　　) (　　) (＊) (　　) (　　) go.
   a. one　　b. have　　c. another

2. (　　) (　　) (＊) (　　) (　　) today.
   a. it　　b. turned　　c. just

3. I'm (　　) (　　) (＊) (　　) (　　) with you.
   a. excited　　b. going　　c. about

4. Well, (　　) (　　) (＊) (　　) (　　) last test tomorrow.
   a. be　　b. after　　c. will

Exercise 3
音声を聴いて、ダイアログの空所 1 ～ 4 を埋めましょう。次に 1 ～ 3 の質問に対する答として最も適切なものを a ～ c の中から選びましょう。

🔊 Audio 1-12

Emily: Are your finals over yet?
定期試験はもう終わった？

Aoi: No, not yet. I have another one to go. What about you? Have you ¹(　　　)(　　　) that report?
まだなの。あと一つよ。あなたは？ レポート書き終わった？

Emily: Yes, I have. As a matter of fact, I just turned it in today.
ええ、終わったわ。実を言うと、今日ちょうど提出したところよ。

Aoi: Good for you. You must be ²(　　　)(　　　) to go back to Perth now, are you? I'm getting excited about going there with you. I've always wanted to go to Australia.
よかったね。じゃあ、パースに戻る準備に取りかかっているよね？ 一緒に行けるからワクワクしてる。オーストラリアにはずっと行きたいと思ってた。

Emily: By the way, have you applied for an ETAS yet? You need to have one to visit Australia.
ところで、ETAS の申請はもう終わった？ オーストラリアに行くには ETAS を取得しておかないと。

Aoi: Yes, I have. It ³(　　　)(　　　) straight away.
申請済みで、もう取得してるわ。

Emily: Good. Now you're all set.
よかった。じゃあ準備万端ね。

Aoi: Well, I will be after the last test tomorrow.
えーっと、明日の最後のテストが終わったら。

Emily: That's right. ⁴(　　　)(　　　) the good work!
そうだったわ。しっかり勉強して！

▶ETAS:「電子渡航許可」制度

1. Has Aoi finished taking her final test?
   a. Yes, she has.　b. No, she hasn't.　c. It's not mentioned.
2. Who is going to Perth?
   a. Aoi　b. Emily　c. Both Aoi and Emily
3. Who applied for an ETAS?
   a. Aoi　b. Emily　c. Both Aoi and Emily

📍 Challenge Corner

ダイアログの音声を聴いて、☐の部分を書き取り、1〜3の質問に対して最も適切な答をa〜cの中から選びましょう。

A week before departure

▶▶▶▶ ◀◀◀◀ 🔊 Audio 1-13

Emily: Where in Australia would you like to go?
Aoi: I don't know much about it. Sydney is the only place I can think of.
Emily: _____, and I loved both places.
Aoi: All right. Then, how about going to Sydney and Cairns, too?

1. Where in Australia has Emily been?
   a. To Sydney   **b.** To Cairns   **c.** To both Sydney and Cairns

▶▶▶▶ ◀◀◀◀ 🔊 Audio 1-14

Emily: _____ in Australia, so you'll need to take some summer clothes.
Aoi: All right. I'll make sure to pack something cool. Thanks for the tip.
Emily: If there's anything else you need to know, please let me know.

2. What's the weather like in Australia at this time of year?
   a. It is cool.   **b.** It is cold.   **c.** It is hot.

▶▶▶▶ ◀◀◀◀ 🔊 Audio 1-15

Emily: They say Victoria Peak has the most beautiful view in Hong Kong.
Aoi: That's what I've heard, too. I can't wait to go there.
Emily: I can show you around Singapore, too _____.

3. Has Emily been to Singapore before?
   a. Yes. Once.   **b.** No. Never.   **c.** Yes. More than once.

英会話で友だちになる

Unit 3 Taiwan: Experiencing Traditional Culture
日常会話―観光

アオイとエミリーの乗った飛行機は台湾へ向けて関西国際空港を出発し、無事に桃園国際空港に到着後、ツアーガイドさんと合流し、貸切のチャーター車で台湾北部にある九份（Jiufen）という山あいの町へ。阿味茶楼（Amei Chajiuguan）で台湾茶を楽しむと、チャーター車で十分（Shifen）へ。

Words & Phrases
次の 1 ～ 10 の語または語句の最も適切な意味を下の a ～ j から選びなさい。

1. Oh, my
2. snappy
3. jade
4. amulet
5. token
6. release
7. lantern
8. nephew
9. celebrate
10. quarter to

a. 翡翠（ヒスイ）
b. 天灯（テントウ）
c. 甥（オイ）
d. ・・・時15分前
e. 祝う
f. あらまあ
g. 記念
h. お守り
i. しゃれた
j. 飛ばす

Warm-up
音声を聴いて、1 ～ 3 のダイアログの空所を埋めましょう。　　Audio 1-16

At the airport

1. **Guide:** Hi! Welcome to Taiwan. I'm your ¹_____, Kuan-Yu Chen.
   Emily: ²_____ to meet you. I'm Emily and this is my friend, Aoi.
   Aoi: Hello. Kuan-Yu. This is our first trip to Taiwan. We're so excited.

In the car

2. **Aoi:** Wow! Look out the window, Emily!
   Emily: What? Oh, my! There are so many ³_____ on the road!
   Guide: You know, Taiwan is known as a motorcycle ⁴_____.

3. **Emily:** Hey, you are wearing a very snappy bracelet!
   Guide: Thanks. It's jade. We Taiwanese ⁵_____ jade as an amulet of good luck.
   Aoi: Cool! Let's get ⁶_____ jade bracelets as a token of this trip, Emily.

Exercise 1　1〜7の(　)内の語または語句を並べかえて英文を完成させましょう。ただし、文頭にくるものも小文字で与えています。次に音声を聴いて答を確認しましょう。

Audio 1-17

1. ただ今、気流の悪いところを飛行中です。
   (currently, experiencing, are, turbulence, we, some, air).
   _____

2. 到着の1時間前に軽食をご用意いたしております。
   (a, will, light, serving, be, we, meal) one hour before arrival.
   _____

3. 晴れた日は石垣島から台湾が見えるそうです。
   They say that on sunny days, (Taiwan, you, Ishigaki Island, can, from, see).
   _____

4. 台湾の国土の約3分の2を山地が占めています。
   (the land, about, mountainous areas, of, two-thirds, account for) of Taiwan.
   _____

5. 台湾で一番高い山は標高3,952メートルです。
   The highest mountain in Taiwan (level, meters, sea, 3,952, is, above).
   _____

6. 九份の丘から眺める海は絶景です。
   The (the top, view, the hill, from, sea, of) in Jiufen is most beautiful.
   _____

7. 九份には昔、金鉱山がありました。
   (to, there, mines, used, gold, be) in Jiufen.
   _____

Exercise 2　1〜4の英文の音声を聴いて、(＊)に入る語をa〜cから選び、記号で答えなさい。

Audio 1-18

1. (　) (　) (＊) (　) (　) in Jiufen are so narrow.
   a. lanes　　b. stone　　c. and

2. I've (　) (　) (＊) (　) (　) with my four-year-old niece.
   a. several　　b. movie　　c. that

3. You can enjoy (　) (　) (＊) (　) (　).
   a. Taiwanese　　b. culture　　c. tea

4. (　) (　) (＊) (　) (　)?
   a. you　　b. salon　　c. do

日常会話 ― 観光

Exercise 3 音声を聴いて、ダイアログの空所 1 〜 4 を埋めましょう。次に 1 〜 3 の質問に対する答として最も適切なものを a 〜 c の中から選びましょう。

🔊 Audio 1-19

Guide: ¹(   ) (   ) (   )! The lanes and stone steps in Jiufen are so narrow and are always very crowded.
足元にお気を付けください！　九份は細道で石段がとても狭いし、いつだって混んでますからね。

Aoi: I really like the retro atmosphere of ²(   ) (   ). I once read somewhere that Jiufen was the setting for the Ghibli movie, *Spirited Away*.
この街並みのレトロな雰囲気すごく気に入ったわ。九份はジブリ映画の「千と千尋の神隠し」の舞台になった街だって、いつかどこかで読んだ気がするわ。

Guide: Right. I've seen that movie several times with my four-year-old niece.
その通りです。私もその映画、4 歳の姪っ子と数回観たことがあります。

Emily: What are those splendid-looking buildings alongside the stone steps?
石段沿いのあの立派な建物はいったいなに？

Guide: They are tea salons. You can enjoy traditional Taiwanese tea culture there.
茶楼です。あそこで伝統的な台湾式のお茶文化を体験できます。

Aoi: I'd love to have some Taiwanese oolong tea. Let's ³(   ) (   ) one of them.
台湾の烏龍茶をぜひ飲んでみたいな。あの茶楼のどれかに立ち寄ろうよ。

Emily: Sure. Why not? Which salon do you recommend?
賛成。どの茶楼がおすすめですか？

Guide: Hmm. How about that one over there? It's very famous.
う〜ん、そうですね。向こうの茶楼はいかがでしょうか？　とても有名な店です。

Emily: Okay! Let's go there. I'm ⁴(   ) (   ) (   ).
了解！　そこに行きましょう。喉がカラカラに乾いちゃったわ。

1. What did the guide say about the lanes and stone steps in Jiufen?
   a. They are so wide.   b. They are so narrow.   c. They are so winding.

2. Who did the guide see the movie, *Spirited Away* with?
   a. His niece   b. His daughter   c. His nephew

3. What are Aoi and Emily most likely to do next?
   a. Drink tea   b. Eat something   c. Go on walking

📍 Challenge Corner

ダイアログの音声を聴いて、▭の部分を書き取り、1～3の質問に対して最も適切な答をa～cの中から選びましょう。

At the Sky Lantern Festival in Shifen

▶▶▶▶ ◀◀◀◀ 🔊 Audio 1-20

Emily: What do you do first before releasing a sky lantern?
Guide: You need to decide the color of lantern you want to release.
Aoi: How many colors are there in total?
Guide: _____ and each color means a different kind of luck.

1. How many colors of lanterns are there?
   a. Seven **b.** Six **c.** Five

▶▶▶▶ ◀◀◀◀ 🔊 Audio 1-21

Guide: Releasing sky lanterns was originally a custom to celebrate a new year.
Emily: Hmm. Is that so?
Guide: Yes. And in the old days, people believed Shifen to be the nearest place to God.
Aoi: I see … Uh-oh, it's beginning to rain. _____.

2. What are they most likely to do next?
   a. Start playing **b.** Go home **c.** Put on their rainwear

In the hotel lobby

▶▶▶▶ ◀◀◀◀ 🔊 Audio 1-22

Guide: Tomorrow we are going to Kaohsiung, the National Palace Museum and Shilin Night Market. So _____.
Aoi: Where are we meeting?
Guide: Right here in the hotel lobby.

➤Kaohsiung：高雄／ Shilin Night Market：士林夜市

3. When are they going to meet tomorrow morning?
   a. At half past seven **b.** At quarter to eight **c.** At quarter past seven

日常会話―観光

Unit 4 Taiwan: Outside Taipei

ツアーガイドとの会話―観光

台北駅から高雄へ向かい、台湾有数のパワースポットの一つ「龍虎塔」で開運祈願。台中で観光後、台北市内に戻り故宮博物館で数々の所蔵品を堪能した後は、台北101に立ち寄り展望台からの景色を満喫。そしていよいよ士林夜市へ出発！　夜市では久しぶりにおいしい台湾バナナを食す。

Words & Phrases 次の 1 ～ 10 の語または語句の最も適切な意味を下の a ～ j から選びなさい。

1. chase away　　2. evil spirit　　3. huge　　4. story
5. exhibit　　6. fantastic　　7. food stall　　8. starter
9. thoroughly　　10. leave for

a. 展示品　　b. すばらしい　　c. 存分に　　d.（食事の）最初に出る料理
e. 悪霊　　f. とても大きい　　g. 追い払う　　h. ・・・（へ向かって）出発する
i.（建物の）階　　j. 屋台

Warm-up 音声を聴いて、1 ～ 3 のダイアログの空所を埋めましょう。   Audio 1-23

1. **Guide:** When visiting the Dragon and Tiger Pagodas, remember to enter
   ¹_____ the dragon's mouth and come out from the tiger's mouth.
   Emily: Really? How come?
   Guide: Well, it's an old tradition. Doing so ²_____ away evil spirits.

2. **Aoi:** Taipei Station is ³_____ huge!
   Emily: You can say that again.
   Guide: It rises six stories ⁴_____ the ground and has four floors underground.

At an ice cream shop

3. **Emily:** Gee! There are more than 60 ⁵_____ of ice cream in this store.
   Aoi: Yeah. And look at that! The store is called *Eye Scream*. There's a huge eyeball in the ice cream cup. So ⁶_____!
   Clerk: May I take your order?

Exercise 1 1～7の（　）内の語または語句を並べかえて英文を完成させましょう。ただし、文頭にくるものも小文字で与えています。次に音声を聴いて答を確認しましょう。

🔊 Audio 1-24

1. 台湾の首都には見どころがたくさんあります。
   There are (capital, must-see, Taiwan, sights, of, the, in, many).
   _____

2. 台湾高速鉄道（THSR）は台北と高雄を結ぶ高速鉄道です。
   THSR is (Taipei, high-speed, with Kaohsiung, linking, train, a).
   _____

3. 烏龍茶は台湾の有名な特産物の一つです。
   (the, of, oolong, most famous, tea, one, specialties, is) of Taiwan.
   _____

4. 国立故宮博物館は世界三大博物館の一つです。
   The National Palace Museum is (largest museums, of, three, the world's, one).
   _____

5. 台湾の夜市はB級グルメの宝庫です。
   The night markets in Taiwan are (of, but tasty, local food, cheap, a trove).
   _____

6. 台湾バナナは1903年に初めて日本に輸出されました。
   Taiwan bananas (first, to, 1903, exported, were, Japan, in).
   _____

7. 国立台湾大学（NTU）は11の学部から成り、3万人を超える学生が通っています。
   NTU (faculties, over, and has, eleven, 30,000 students, comprises).
   _____

Exercise 2 1～4の音声を聴いて、（ * ）に入る語をa～cから選び、記号で答えなさい。

🔊 Audio 1-25

1. Do you want to (　) (　) (*) (　) (　)?
   a. up　　**b.** a　　**c.** for

2. (　) (　) (*) (　) (　) LINE, OK?
   a. touch　**b.** in　**c.** keep

3. Did you go to the (　) (　) (*) (　) (　) section?
   a. and　　**b.** Genre　**c.** Paintings

4. (　) (　) (*) (　) (　) again.
   a. go　　**b.** back　　**c.** should

Exercise 3 音声を聴いて、空所 1 〜 4 を埋めましょう。次に 1 〜 3 の質問に対する答として最も適切なものを a 〜 c の中から選びましょう。

🔊 Audio 1-26

At the National Palace Museum

Emily: I'd like to see the *Jade Cabbage* and the *Meat-shaped Stone* once more. How about you, Aoi?
私はもう一度「翠玉白菜」と「肉形石」を見たいな。あなたはどう、アオイ？

Aoi: The *Emperor's Furniture* was fascinating. I want to see that again.
「皇帝の家具」が魅力的だったわ。あれをまた見たいな。

Emily: Do you want to split up for a bit?
ほんの少し別行動する？

Aoi: Sure. Let's keep in touch by LINE, OK?
了解。LINE で連絡を取り続けようね。

Chatting on LINE

Aoi
I was so impressed by the ¹(   ) (   ) of potteries. They're great art works.
膨大な数の陶磁器のコレクションにとっても感動したわ。素晴らしい芸術作品よ。

Emily
Yeah. They're ²(   ) (   ). By the way, did you go to the Landscape Paintings and Genre Paintings section?
本当ね。息を呑むような見事さだもの。ところで、山水画と風俗画のコーナーへは行った？

Aoi
I did. But I couldn't ³(   ) (   ) because it was so crowded.
うん。でも大勢の見物客がいたから何も見えなかった。

Emily
You should go back there again. Every picture is ⁴(   ) (   ).
もう一度そのコーナーへ戻るべきよ。どの絵画もとっても感動的なんだから。

1. What does Emily want to see once more?
   a. All the exhibits
   b. The *Emperor's Furniture*
   c. The *Jade Cabbage* and the *Meat-shaped Stone*

2. Who went to see the huge collection of potteries?
   a. Aoi   b. Emily   c. Both Aoi and Emily

3. Aoi saw landscape paintings and genre paintings, didn't she?
   a. Yes, she did.   b. No, she didn't.   c. It's not mentioned.

📍 Challenge Corner

ダイアログの音声を聴いて、⬜ の部分を書き取り、1～3の質問に対して最も適切な答をa～cの中から選びましょう。

On the observation deck of Taipei 101

▶▶▶▶ ◀◀◀◀ 🔊 Audio 1-27

Aoi: What a fantastic view!
Emily: Isn't it cool? I wonder how long it took us to get up here in the elevator.
Guide: Good question! _____, though we're 89 floors up.

1. How much time did it take to get up to the 89th floor by elevator?
   a. 13 seconds   **b.** 30 seconds   **c.** 37 seconds

At Shilin Night Market

▶▶▶▶ ◀◀◀◀ 🔊 Audio 1-28

Emily: There are so many food stalls here.
Aoi: _____ starters?
Emily: Let's eat pepper pie and oyster omelet over there!

2. Who will most likely eat pepper pie and oyster omelet?
   a. Aoi   **b.** Emily   **c.** Both Aoi and Emily

In the hotel lounge

▶▶▶▶ ◀◀◀◀ 🔊 Audio 1-29

Aoi: We've had a thoroughly enjoyable time here in Taiwan, haven't we?
Emily: Yeah, but we didn't have enough time to go to Taroko Valley this time. So let's go there next time.
Aoi: Yep, let's do that. _____.

3. Where will Aoi and Emily be leaving for tomorrow?
   a. Shanghai   **b.** Hong Kong   **c.** Singapore

Unit 5 Hong Kong: What a Wonderful Night View!

日常会話＋eメールで―観光

アオイは今回のエミリーとの旅行をサンフランシスコのジュディにメールで知らせる。アオイとエミリーは香港到着後、おいしい飲茶を堪能し、ネイザンロードを散策後、ビクトリアピーク・ツアーに参加して香港の百万ドルの夜景やシンフォニー・オブ・ライツを満喫。

Words & Phrases
次の1～10の語または語句の最も適切な意味を下のa～jから選びなさい。

1. hang out
2. catch up with
3. on business
4. over
5. red-brick
6. artificial
7. keep in touch
8. itinerary
9. complimentary
10. dim sum

a. 赤レンガ　　b. 点心　　c. 人工の　　d. 無料の
e. 近況報告を聞く　f. ・・・の間　g. 旅程(表)　h. ぶらぶらして時を過ごす
i. 商用で　　j. またお便りをください

Warm-up
音声を聴いて、1～3のダイアログの空所を埋めましょう。　　🔊 Audio 1-30

At the airport

1. **Emily:** Where in Hong Kong is our ¹_____?
   Aoi: Let's see ... it's in Kowloon.
   Emily: Is it ²_____ Nathan Road?

In the hotel lobby

2. **Emily:** We're seeing *A Symphony of Lights* ³_____ tonight, right?
   Aoi: That's right. We're going to enjoy it from Victoria Peak.
   Emily: Good. I'm sure it'll be ⁴_____.

3. **Aoi:** I'd like to ⁵_____ out at a night market.
   Emily: Then we should go to Tung Choi Street.
   Aoi: How can we ⁶_____ there from our hotel?

Exercise 1　1〜7の（　）内の語または語句を並べかえて英文を完成させましょう。ただし、文頭にくるものも小文字で与えています。次に音声を聴いて答を確認しましょう。

🔊 Audio 1-31

1. 台湾から香港まで2時間弱のフライトです。
   (two hours, air, takes, less than, by, it, a little) from Taiwan to Hong Kong.
   _____

2. 九龍から香港島まではフェリーで行くのをおすすめします。
   I (from, the ferry, to, Kowloon, recommend) Hong Kong Island.
   _____

3. ビクトリアピークから香港の素晴らしい景色を楽しめます。
   You can (a wonderful, Hong Kong, enjoy, of, view) from Victoria Peak.
   _____

4. 香港はアヘン戦争後にイギリスに割譲されました。
   Hong Kong (the United Kingdom, was, to, after, ceded, the Opium Wars).
   _____

5. ザ・ペニンシュラ香港は香港でもっとも素晴らしいホテルの一つです。
   The Peninsula Hong Kong (the, Hong Kong, one, hotels, is, finest, of, in).
   _____

6. 香港の人口密度はとても高いです。
   (high, has, Hong Kong, extremely, density, an, population).
   _____

7. 私たちは香港からマカオまで日帰り旅行を計画しています。
   We (Macau, planning, trip, a, to, are, day) from Hong Kong.
   _____

Exercise 2　1〜4の英文の音声を聴いて、（ * ）に入る語をa〜cから選び、記号で答えなさい。

🔊 Audio 1-32

1. (　　) (　　) (*) (　　) (　　) father.
   a. with　　b. up　　c. caught

2. (　　) (　　) (*) (　　) (　　) Park.
   a. jogging　　b. in　　c. went

3. (　　) (　　) (*) (　　) (　　) Boston.
   a. took　　b. train　　c. a

4. (　　), (　　) (*) (　　) (　　)?
   a. it　　b. is　　c. how

Exercise 3　次の電子メールを読んで以下の質問に答えましょう。

Dear Aoi,

I was in New York with my mom for a week. While there, we caught up with my father over the weekend since he is there [1](　　　)(　　　). We went to Fifth Avenue, Times Square, and the Statue of Liberty, among other places. I went jogging in Central Park since our hotel was near there. Central Park is a huge, artificial park and was the [2](　　　)(　　　)(　　　) created in the US.

This time we took a train to Boston and stayed there for a few days. When we saw red-brick buildings, Boston Tea Party Ships, and Harvard University, we really [3](　　　)(　　　)(　　　) for its history. I remembered Boston was where the War of Independence broke out in 1775.

You must be in Hong Kong today, [4](　　　)(　　　) your itinerary. Well, how is it there? I'll LINE you later, so you can tell me what you've been up to.

Please keep in touch,

Judy

Q1 音声を聴いて、Email の空所 1〜4 を埋めましょう。　　Audio 1-33

Q2 Email の内容について、音声を聴き最も適切な答を a〜c の中から選びましょう。

Audio 1-33

1. Who did Judy go to New York with?
   a. Her friend　　b. Her father　　c. Her mother

2. Where did Judy jog?
   a. In Times Square　　b. In Central Park　　c. On Fifth Avenue

3. When did the War of Independence begin?
   a. In 1775　　b. In 1776　　c. In 1777

📍 Challenge Corner

ダイアログの音声を聴いて、_____の部分を書き取り、1〜3の質問に対して最も適切な答をa〜cの中から選びましょう。

At Hong Kong International Airport

▶▶▶▶ ◀◀◀◀ 🔊 Audio 1-34

Emily: Let's check in at the hotel first and ask them to keep our luggage.

Aoi: Good idea. Our hotel is in Kowloon, right?

Emily: Yes. I've heard _____ from the airport.

1. How are Aoi and Emily most likely getting to the hotel?
   a. By taxi　　　b. By car　　　c. By shuttle bus

In the hotel lobby

▶▶▶▶ ◀◀◀◀ 🔊 Audio 1-35

Emily: Excuse me. Are there any good dim sum restaurants near the hotel?

Concierge: Sure. I recommend this one. _____.

Emily: Thanks. Could you show me how to get there?

2. How far is it to the dim sum restaurant from the hotel?
   a. Only five minutes by taxi
   b. Only five minutes by bus
   c. Only five minutes on foot

At a café on Nathan Road

▶▶▶▶ ◀◀◀◀ 🔊 Audio 1-36

Aoi: It's about time we got back to the hotel _____.

Emily: All right. We don't want to miss it, so let's hurry back.

Aoi: You know you can even see *A Symphony of Lights* show from the Peak.

3. Why are Aoi and Emily going back to the hotel?
   a. To ask about the Victoria Peak tour
   b. To join the Victoria Peak tour
   c. To climb up Victoria Peak

Unit 6　Hong Kong: Dinner on a Floating Restaurant?

日常会話＋SNSで―観光

今日はフェリーで香港島にわたり、下町風情が残る「上環」から高層ビルが立ち並ぶ金融と商業の中心の「中環」まで歩いて回る。アバディーンの水上レストランで夕食を食べ、ホテルに戻ってロビーの側にあるラウンジでくつろいでいた時、サンフランシスコのジュディからLINEが入る。

Words & Phrases　次の1～10の語または語句の最も適切な意味を下のa～jから選びなさい。

1. tram　　　　2. extend　　　　3. exact　　　　4. figure
5. million　　　6. especially　　 7. make it　　　 8. every minute of it
9. by the way　10. get around

　　a. 数字　　　　　b. 百万　　　　　c. ケーブルカー　　d. あちこちに移動する
　　e. 正確な　　　　f. 特に　　　　　g. 延ばす　　　　　h. ところで
　　i. やりくりする　 j. 終始

Warm-up　音声を聴いて、1～3のダイアログの空所を埋めましょう。　　　Audio 1-37

1. **Emily:** Do you know how high Victoria [1]_____ is?
   Aoi: No, I don't. How high is it?
   Emily: It's 552 meters high. You can get up to the top by [2]_____.

2. **Aoi:** We won't be going to Macau because we don't have enough time.
   Emily: Too bad. I wish we had [3]_____ day here.
   Aoi: Well, would you like to [4]_____ our stay by one more night?

3. **Aoi:** What's the population of Hong Kong?
   Emily: I know a lot of people live here, but I don't know the [5]_____ figure.
   Aoi: Oh, look here. It says it's about 7.3 [6]_____.

Exercise 1
1〜7の（　）内の語または語句を並べかえて英文を完成させましょう。ただし、文頭にくるものも小文字で与えています。次に音声を聴いて答を確認しましょう。

Audio 1-38

1. スターフェリーは地元の人々に人気があります。
   The Star Ferry is (the, a, among, locals, favorite).

2. 多くの旅行客がオープントップバスツアーで香港の素晴らしい景色を堪能します。
   Many tourists (great, of, an open-top bus tour, sights, enjoy, Hong Kong's).

3. 中国は1887年にポルトガルによるマカオの支配を認めました。
   China (Portuguese, Macau, control, recognized, of) in 1887.

4. 聖ポール天主堂跡はマカオのシンボルです。
   (the, of, are, a, of, symbol, St. Paul's Cathedral, Macau, ruins).

5. マカオはカジノだけでなく30もの世界遺産で有名です。
   Macau is (its 30 World Heritage sites, its casinos, famous, but, not only for).

6. 香港ディズニーランドはランタオ島にあるテーマパークです。
   Hong Kong Disneyland (located, theme park, is, Lantau Island, a, on).

7. 私たちはアバディーンの水上レストランで夕食に海鮮料理を食べました。
   We (dinner, restaurant, had, a, seafood, for, floating, on) in Aberdeen.

Exercise 2
1〜4の英文の音声を聴いて、（ ＊ ）に入る語をa〜cから選び、記号で答えなさい。

Audio 1-39

1. (　　)(　　)(＊)(　　)(　　) enjoy *A Symphony of Lights* show!
   a. we　　　　**b.** lucky　　　**c.** to

2. You find (　　)(　　)(＊)(　　)(　　).
   a. street　　**b.** lot　　　　**c.** of

3. I (　　)(　　)(＊)(　　)(　　), too.
   a. for　　　　**b.** some　　　**c.** my

4. (　　)(　　)(＊)(　　)(　　) to Central.
   a. Star　　　**b.** a　　　　　**c.** take

Exercise 3 音声を聴いて、ダイアログの空所 1 ～ 4 を埋めましょう。次に 1 ～ 3 の質問に対する答として最も適切なものを a ～ c の中から選びましょう。

🔊 **Audio 1-40**

Emily: The night view of Hong Kong from Victoria Peak was ¹(　　　) (　　　) (　　　).
ビクトリア・ピークから見た香港の夜景は本当にすごかったわ。

Aoi: Oh, yes. And how lucky we were to enjoy *A Symphony of Lights* show from there! That was gorgeous, too.
ああ、そうね。それに、そこからシンフォニー・オブ・ライツの光と音のショーを見ることができてなんてラッキーだったんだろう！　そのショーもすてきだった。

Emily: It sure was. It's recognized as one of the world's ²(　　　) (　　　) light shows.
確かにすごかった。それは世界で最も見ごたえのある光のショーの一つと認められているのよ。

Aoi: I can see why. And Tung Choi Street in Mong Kok also interested me.
わかるわ。それから旺角の女人街もとても興味深かった。

Emily: Yeah. You find a lot of street stalls with a ³(　　　) (　　　) (　　　) there. I ⁴(　　　) (　　　) (　　　) some gifts for my friends back home.
そうね。あそこにはいろんな物を売ってる屋台が立ち並んでいたわね。故郷の友だちへのお土産を買わずにはいられなかった。

Aoi: Right. I bought some for my friends, too.
そうね。私も友だちへのお土産をいくつか買っちゃった。

Emily: By the way, we are going to Sheung Wan and Central in Hong Kong Island today, aren't we?
ところで、今日は香港島の上環と中環に行くんだよね？

Aoi: We sure are. From Kowloon we'll take a Star Ferry to Central, and walk to Sheung Wan.
そうよ。九龍からはスターフェリーで中環まで行って、それから歩いて上環まで行く予定よ。

1. Where did Aoi and Emily go last night?
   a. Victoria Peak, *A Symphony of Lights*, and Tung Choi Street
   b. Victoria Street and *A Symphony of Lights*
   c. Victoria Peak and Tung Choi Street
2. Who bought some gifts on Tung Choi Street?
   a. Aoi
   b. Emily
   c. Both Aoi and Emily
3. How will Aoi and Emily go to Hong Kong Island?
   a. By taxi.
   b. By ferry
   c. By air

Challenge Corner

ダイアログの音声を聴いて、■の部分を書き取り、1～3の質問に対して最も適切な答をa～cの中から選びましょう。

🔊 Audio 1-41

Aoi
We went to Victoria Peak, a floating restaurant, and a night market.

Judy
Did you go to Hong Kong Disneyland?

Aoi
No. _____ since we didn't have enough time.

1. Did Aoi and Emily go to Hong Kong Disneyland?

   a. Yes, they did.   **b.** No, they didn't.   **c.** It's not mentioned.

In the hotel room

▶▶▶▶ ◀◀◀◀   🔊 Audio 1-42

Emily: _____, didn't we? My feet are killing me.
Aoi: So are mine, but I enjoyed every minute of it.
Emily: So did I. I especially liked dinner on a floating restaurant.

2. How did Aoi and Emily get around today?

   a. By taxi   **b.** On foot   **c.** By bus

▶▶▶▶ ◀◀◀◀   🔊 Audio 1-43

Emily: Next time I want to go to Hong Kong Disneyland and Macau.
Aoi: Me, too. By the way, what time is our flight to Singapore tomorrow?
Emily: Let's see … it's at 11:30 a.m., so _____.

3. What time will Aoi and Emily be leaving the hotel?

   a. At 7:30 a.m.   **b.** At 8:30 a.m.   **c.** At 11:30 a.m.

日常会話＋SNSで―観光

Unit 7 At Hong Kong International Airport: A New Friend

到着後の空港では―初対面の人と英語で話す

アオイとエミリーはシンガポールに向かうため出発2時間半ほど前に香港国際空港に到着。そこでオーストラリアのアデレード出身のジャックと知り合う。彼は大阪や京都には行ったことはあるが神戸に行ったことはない。アデレードの大学を卒業後、日本で英語を教えたいとの夢を抱いている。

Words & Phrases
次の1〜10の語または語句の最も適切な意味を下のa〜jから選びなさい。

1. transit lounge
2. in transit
3. connecting flight
4. behind
5. temple
6. another
7. depart for
8. proceed to
9. be supposed to
10. original

a. 寺
b. ・・・に向けて出発する
c. ・・・へ進む
d. 本来の
e. 接続便
f. 別の
g. 移動中で
h. 乗り継ぎ用待合室
i. ・・・のうしろに
j. ・・・をすることになっている

Warm-up
音声を聴いて、1〜3のダイアログの空所を埋めましょう。 Audio 1-44

In the transit lounge, just after passport control

1. **Aoi:** Excuse me for a ¹_____. I need to go to the bathroom.
   Emily: Sure. Do you know where it is?
   Aoi: Yes. I just saw one right ²_____ us.

2. **Emily:** Are you in ³_____ here?
   Jack: Yes, I am. I'm waiting for my ⁴_____ flight to Tokyo. And you?
   Emily: I'm waiting for my flight to Singapore.

3. **Emily:** Where are you from, Jack?
   Jack: I'm from Adelaide, ⁵_____ Australia.
   Emily: Adelaide. I've never ⁶_____ there. What's it like?

Exercise 1
1～7の(　)内の語または語句を並べかえて英文を完成させましょう。ただし、文頭にくるものも小文字で与えています。次に音声を聴いて答を確認しましょう。

Audio 1-45

1. チェックインはすでに始まっているようです。
   (already, that, started, it, check-in, has, seems).

   _____

2. 出発2時間前に搭乗手続きするようになっています。
   You are (to, two hours, departure, supposed, before, check in).

   _____

3. 私は朝早く起きたのでちょっと眠いです。
   I'm (got, I, a bit, this morning, since, early, up, sleepy).

   _____

4. そのカフェはとても混んでいましたが、彼女たちは幸運にも空いてる席を見つけることができました。
   That café was (but luckily, able, they, a table, to, were, very busy, find).

   _____

5. 香港国際空港にはシャワーを浴びるところがあります。
   You (a, can, at, shower, take) Hong Kong International Airport.

   _____

6. 東京便は30分遅れるとのアナウンスがありました。
   They announced (be, 30 minutes, would, the flight, delayed, to Tokyo).

   _____

7. 香港には貨物取扱量が世界で最も多い空港があります。
   Hong Kong has (by, airport, the world's, cargo traffic, busiest).

   _____

Exercise 2
1～4の英文の音声を聴いて、(*)に入る語をa～cから選び、記号で答えなさい。

Audio 1-46

1. I'm going to Yokohama (　) (　) (*) (　) (　).
   a. visit   **b.** friends   **c.** some

2. (　) (　) (*) (　) (　) in Kobe.
   a. studying   **b.** been   **c.** Japanese

3. (　) (　) (*) (　) (　).
   a. recommend   **b.** visit   **c.** you

4. (　) (　) (*) (　) (　) to Yokohama.
   a. way   **b.** on   **c.** is

Exercise 3 音声を聴いて、ダイアログの空所 1 ～ 4 を埋めましょう。次に 1 ～ 3 の質問に対する答として最も適切なものを a ～ c の中から選びましょう。

🔊 Audio 1-47

In the transit lounge

Emily: ¹( ) ( ) ( ) are you going, Jack?
日本のどこに行くんですか、ジャック。

Jack: I'm going to Yokohama to visit some Japanese friends. I studied Japanese for a year at university there.
日本の友人を訪問するために横浜に行きます。そこにある大学で日本語を 1 年間勉強したことがあります。

Emily: Really? I've been studying Japanese culture in Kobe for ²( ) ( ) ( ).
本当ですか？ 私は 8 か月ほど神戸で日本文化の研究をしています。

Jack: I've never been to Kobe, but I've been to Kyoto and Osaka once.
神戸には行ったことはありませんが、京都と大阪は一度行ったことがあります。

Emily: Kobe is a ³( ) ( ) ( ). When you have time, I recommend you visit there. By the way, have you been to Singapore before?
神戸はとてもすてきな街です。時間のあったらそこに行くことをおすすめします。ところで、シンガポールに以前行ったことはありますか？

Jack: Yes, I have. I've been there twice. It's a great place. I liked it very much.
はい。2 度行ったことがあります。すばらしいところで、私は大好きです。

Aoi returns from window-shopping

Emily: Aoi, this is Jack. He's from Adelaide, Australia. He's ⁴( ) ( ) here and is on his way to Yokohama to see his friends.
アオイ、こちらはジャック。オーストラリアのアデレード出身。彼は飛行機の乗り換えでここにいて、友だちに会いに横浜に行くんだって。

Jack: Nice to meet you, Aoi.
初めまして、アオイ。

1. How long did Jack study Japanese at university in Yokohama?
   a. For one month   b. For one year   c. For three years

2. Where in the Kansai area has Jack been?
   a. Kyoto   b. Kyoto and Osaka   c. Kyoto, Osaka, and Kobe

3. Has Jack ever been to Singapore?
   a. Yes. Once.   b. Yes. Twice.   c. Yes. More than twice.

📍 Challenge Corner

ダイアログの音声を聴いて、　　の部分を書き取り、1〜3の質問に対して最も適切な答をa〜cの中から選びましょう。

▶▶▶▶ ◀◀◀◀　　　　　　　　　　🔊 Audio 1-48

Jack: _____.

Emily: You've traveled a lot, haven't you? Did you like those places?

Jack: Sure. I did some sightseeing in Ho Chi Minh City, and I think I visited just about all the famous temples in Bangkok.

1. How many countries has Jack been to?
   a. Two　　　　　b. Three　　　　　c. Four

An announcement

▶▶▶▶ ◀◀◀◀　　　　　　　　　　🔊 Audio 1-49

Nippon Airlines _____ is now ready for boarding. Passengers for this flight, please proceed to Gate 45.

Aoi: Was that announcement for Flight 76 for Tokyo?

Jack: No. It was for another flight.

2. What was the announcement for?
   a. Flight 76　　　b. Flight 79　　　c. Flight 45

At the check-in counter

▶▶▶▶ ◀◀◀◀　　　　　　　　　　🔊 Audio 1-50

Jack: _____ and it's 10:30 now. Why hasn't boarding started?

Attendant: What is your flight number, Sir?

Jack: Flight 76 to Tokyo.

Attendant: Sorry Sir, but the boarding time has been changed to 10:50.

3. What time was Jack's original boarding time?
   a. 10:20　　　　b. 10:30　　　　c. 10:50

到着後の空港では—初対面の人と英語で話す

Unit 8 Thailand: The Land of Smiles
機内では―観光

アオイとエミリーのシンガポール便は搭乗ゲートが変更になったものの無事出発。香港からシンガポールまでおよそ4時間の空の旅。ジャックから聞いた話に興味を持った二人は機会があればタイとベトナムに行きたいと思うようになる。機内で4時間ほど楽しく過ごした後、シンガポールに到着。

Words & Phrases
次の1～10の語または語句の最も適切な意味を下のa～jから選びなさい。

1. keep one's fingers crossed
2. might as well
3. boarding pass
4. ahead of
5. colonial architecture
6. quite a lot
7. former
8. exit
9. overhead compartment
10. on time

a. 予定より早く
b. 植民地時代の建築物
c. 時間通りに
d. 幸運を祈る
e. 頭上の荷物入れ
f. ・・・したほうがいい
g. 搭乗券
h. 前の
i. かなり多くの
j. 退去する

##
音声を聴いて、1～3のダイアログの空所を埋めましょう。　　Audio 1-51

In the transit lounge

1. **Aoi:** I just hope Jack gets that English-teaching job in Japan.
   Emily: So do I. I remember him saying he had a pretty good ¹_____ of getting it.
   Aoi: Well, let's keep our ²_____ crossed.

2. **Emily:** It's about time they made a boarding announcement for our flight.
   Aoi: Right. We might as well get ³_____ for boarding.
   Emily: OK. I have my boarding pass and ⁴_____. Do I need anything else?

An announcement

3. Passengers on Hong Kong Airlines ⁵_____ 136 to Singapore, your flight is now boarding at Gate 81.
   Emily: All right. Let's get going in ⁶_____ not to be late.

Exercise 1
1〜7の（　）内の語または語句を並べかえて英文を完成させましょう。ただし、文頭にくるものも小文字で与えています。次に音声を聴いて答を確認しましょう。

🔊 Audio 1-52

1. 私たちは搭乗ゲートが変更になっていたなんて知りませんでした。
We (gate, didn't, changed, had been, know, the).
_____

2. こちらは香港航空シンガポール行き136便の最終案内でございます。
(Hong Kong Airlines Flight 136, is, Singapore, call, the, for, final, to, this).
_____

3. お客様のエミリー・アトキンス様、案内デスクまでお越しください。
(to, passenger, the information desk, Emily Atkins, would, please report)?
_____

4. シンガポールまでの飛行時間は約4時間を予定しております。
(Singapore, be, flight time, to, the, expected, is, to) about 4 hours.
_____

5. 到着するまであとどれくらいかかりますか。
(be, much, will, it, how, longer) before we arrive?
_____

6. コーヒーのお代わりをいただけますか。
(of, have, coffee, I, another, can, cup)?
_____

7. 香港は東京よりもシンガポールに近いです。
Hong Kong is (than, it is, closer, to Tokyo, to Singapore).
_____

Exercise 2
1〜4の英文の音声を聴いて、（　＊　）に入る語をa〜cから選び、記号で答えなさい。

🔊 Audio 1-53

1. Talking with Jack (　　) (　　) (　＊　) (　　) (　　) to Thailand.
　a. want　　b. to　　c. me

2. I just (　　) (　　) (　＊　) (　　) (　　) Internet.
　a. on　　b. it　　c. up

3. It's (　　) (　　) (　＊　) (　　) (　　).
　a. for　　b. its　　c. ancient

4. You know, (　　) (　　) (　＊　) (　　) (　　).
　a. a　　b. have　　c. still

Exercise 3　音声を聴いて、ダイアログの空所 1 ～ 4 を埋めましょう。次に 1 ～ 3 の質問に対する答として最も適切なものを a ～ c の中から選びましょう。

🔊 Audio 1-54

On the plane

Emily: Talking with Jack makes me want to go to Thailand.
ジャックと話して、タイに行きたくなったわ。

Aoi: Same here, so I just looked it up on the Internet and found many interesting places.
私も。それでネットでタイのことをちょっと調べたら、興味深い場所がたくさんあったわ。

Emily: Such as?
例えば？

Aoi: The Temple of the Emerald Buddha, the Temple of Dawn in Bangkok, and the Ayutthaya Ruins. Chiang Mai [1](　　　)(　　　)(　　　).
バンコクにあるエメラルド寺院や暁の寺、そしてアユタヤの遺跡。チェンマイも興味深いのよね。

Emily: Chiang Mai? What's that?
チェンマイ？　何それ？

Aoi: It's a city about 700 kilometers north of Bangkok. It's famous for its ancient temples, beautiful Thai silk, and a night bazaar, [2](　　　)(　　　)(　　　).
バンコクから北に約 700 キロのところにある街。古いお寺や美しいタイシルク、そしてとりわけ夜市で有名よ。

Emily: You know, they still have a king, so the [3](　　　)(　　　) of Thailand is the Kingdom of Thailand, right?
ところで、タイにはまだ王様がいるから、タイの正式名称はタイ王国だよね？

Aoi: That's right. The [4](　　　)(　　　)(　　　) to be helpful, courteous, and kind. Thailand is often called the "Land of Smiles."
その通り。地元の人たちは助けになってくれて、礼儀正しく、優しいことで知られているのよ。タイはよく「微笑みの国」と呼ばれているわ。

1. Who wants to go to Thailand?
   a. Aoi　　　　**b.** Emily　　　　**c.** Both Aoi and Emily
2. What city is famous for its beautiful Thai silk?
   a. Ayutthaya　　　　**b.** Bankok　　　　**c.** Chiang Mai
3. What is Thailand often called?
   a. The "Land of Smiles"　　**b.** The "King's Land"　　**c.** The "Land of Temples"

📍 Challenge Corner

ダイアログの音声を聴いて、　　の部分を書き取り、1〜3の質問に対して最も適切な答をa〜cの中から選びましょう。

On the plane

▶▶▶▶ ◀◀◀◀　　　🔊 Audio 1-55

Aoi: Phuket is famous for its beach resorts.
Emily: _____ on holiday.
Aoi: How nice! Next time we come down this way, we should go there.

1. Who has been to Phuket?
   a. Some of Aoi's friends　　b. Some of Emily's friends　　c. Aoi and Emily

▶▶▶▶ ◀◀◀◀　　　🔊 Audio 1-56

Aoi: Is Saigon the former name of Ho Chi Ming City?
Emily: Yes, it is. _____ from Saigon to Ho Chi Minh City in 1975.
Aoi: And "Paris of the Orient" is its nickname, isn't it?
Emily: Right. It was once under the control of France and you can still see quite a lot of French colonial architecture there. That's why.

2. When did Saigon become Ho Chi Ming City?
   a. In 1775　　　　b. In 1875　　　　c. In 1975

An announcement just before leaving the aircraft

▶▶▶▶ ◀◀◀◀　　　🔊 Audio 1-57

Ladies and Gentlemen, please exit from the two doors at the front of the cabin. Please check around your seat and in the overhead compartment to make sure you do not leave anything behind.

Emily: Here we are, Singapore. _____ .

3. Did the plane arrive in Singapore on time?
   a. No. It arrived behind schedule.
   b. No. It arrived ahead of schedule.
   c. Yes, it did.

Unit 9 Singapore: A Multiethnic Society

ツアーガイドとの会話―観光

アオイとエミリーはシンガポールのチャンギ国際空港に到着。シンガポールではガイドさん付きの半日観光を予約していた。ガイドさんからマリーナ地区やリトルインディア、そしてアラブストリートなどを案内してもらいながら、二人はシンガポールの多文化共存社会を体験する。

Words & Phrases

次の1～10の語または語句の最も適切な意味を下のa～jから選びなさい。

1. immigration
2. orchid
3. display board
4. be right back
5. far from
6. recommend
7. high tea
8. on foot
9. most likely
10. nearby

a. 徒歩で
b. すすめる
c. …から遠い
d. 近くに
e. たぶん
f. ラン（の花）
g. 入国審査
h. 表示板
i. すぐに戻る
j. 夕方早くとる軽い食事

Warm-up

音声を聴いて、1～3のダイアログの空所を埋めましょう。　　Audio 2-01

Near immigration

1. **Emily:** Look at those orchids. Aren't they ¹_____?
   Aoi: They sure are. I love orchids.
   Emily: Singapore's ²_____ flower is a variety of orchid, you know.

At the arrival gate

2. **Emily:** That guy over there must be our tour guide.
   Aoi: Which one? The guy with the ³_____ board?
   Emily: Yes. Our names are ⁴_____ on the board he's holding.

3. **Emily:** Hello. I'm Emily Atkins. Are you the tour guide?
   Guide: Yes. I'm Michael Chang ⁵_____ Star Tours. Is Ms Aoi Manabe here?
   Emily: Yes. She'll be ⁶_____ back.

Exercise 1　1〜7の（　）内の語または語句を並べかえて英文を完成させましょう。ただし、文頭にくるものも小文字で与えています。次に音声を聴いて答を確認しましょう。

Audio 2-02

1. 私たちはシンガポールの半日観光に申し込んでいます。
   (for, signed, a half-day, up, tour, we've) of Singapore.
   _____

2. シンガポールは多民族国家として知られています。
   (multiethnic, known, Singapore, nation, as, a, is).
   _____

3. シンガポールはマレーシアと分離し、1965年に独立国家となりました。
   Singapore (Malaysia, became, separated, and, independent, from) in 1965.
   _____

4. そのフードコートでは新鮮でとてもおいしい海鮮料理を手頃な値段で食べることができます。
   You can eat (price, and delicious, at, seafood, reasonable, a, fresh) at the food court.
   _____

5. シンガポールの国土面積は淡路島とほぼ同じくらいです。
   Singapore (about, size, as, is, same, the) Awaji Island.
   _____

6. ラッフルズホテルは1887年に設立され、トーマス・ラッフルズ卿にちなんで名付けられています。
   The Raffles was (Sir Thomas Raffles, in 1887, and named, established, after).
   _____

7. シンガポールでは水不足はとても深刻な問題です。
   (a, the shortage, problem, is, of, serious, water, very) in Singapore.
   _____

Exercise 2　1〜4の英文の音声を聴いて、（　*　）に入る語をa〜cから選び、記号で答えなさい。

Audio 2-03

1. (　　) (　　) (　*　) (　　) (　　) rotation of the Flyer take?
   a. does　　b. time　　c. one

2. Is the (　　) (　　) (　*　) (　　) (　　) hotel?
   a. our　　b. far　　c. from

3. (　　), (　　) (　*　) (　　) (　　).
   a. far　　b. that　　c. not

4. (　　) (　　) (　*　) (　　) (　　) bus there.
   a. get　　b. don't　　c. off

ツアーガイドとの会話 ― 観光

Exercise 3

音声を聴いて、ダイアログの空所 1 ～ 4 を埋めましょう。次に 1 ～ 3 の質問に対する答として最も適切なものを a ～ c の中から選びましょう。

🔊 Audio 2-04

On the tour bus

Guide: We're going to see the Merlion in Marina Bay first. From there you can take in ¹(　　　)(　　　)(　　　) the Marina Bay Sands and the Singapore Flyer.
私たちはまずマリーナベイにあるマーライオンを見に行きます。そこからマリーナベイ・サンズやシンガポールフライヤーがよく見えますよ。

Aoi: Cool. How long does one rotation of the Flyer take?
すごい。そのフライヤーが一周するのにどれくらい時間がかかるんですか？

Guide: It takes about 30 minutes.
30 分くらいです。

Aoi: That long, huh? Is the Singapore Flyer far from our hotel?
そんなに長いんですか？ シンガポールフライヤーは私たちのホテルからは遠いんですか？

Guide: From your hotel … no, it's not that far. Actually it's ²(　　　)(　　　)(　　　).
あなた方のホテルからだったら……それほど遠くありません。実際のところ、歩いて行けるところにあります。

Emily: By the way, can you swim in the ³(　　　)(　　　) at the Marina Bay Sands Hotel?
ところで、マリーナベイ・サンズ・ホテルの屋上にあるプールで泳げますか？

Guide: You can, but only when you are staying at the hotel.
はい、でも宿泊客だけです。

A couple of hours later

Guide: Now we're going to Little India and Arab Street.
さて、リトルインディアとアラブストリートに行きましょう。

Emily: Sounds good. Are we going to Orchard Road as well?
いいですね。オーチャード通りにも行きますか？

Guide: Yes, but you don't get off the bus there. We'll ⁴(　　　)(　　　)(　　　).
はい、でもそこではバスを降りません。車窓からの見学となります。

1. Where is the Merlion?
   a. It's in the Singapore Flyer.
   b. It's in the Marina Bay area.
   c. It's in the Marina Bay Sands.

2. Is the hotel Aoi and Emily are staying at far from the Singapore Flyer?
   a. No, it's not.   b. Yes, it is.   c. Yes, it's not that far.

3. Are Aoi and Emily getting off the bus at Orchard Road?
   a. Yes, they are.   b. No, they aren't.   c. It's not mentioned.

Challenge Corner

ダイアログの音声を聴いて、▨の部分を書き取り、1～3の質問に対して最も適切な答をa～cの中から選びましょう。

Driving along Orchard Road

▶▶▶▶ ◀◀◀◀ 🔊 Audio 2-05

Guide: OK. We're going to go back to Marina Bay now and check in at the hotel.
Aoi: _____?
Guide: Sure. They are quite a few of them nearby. Both locals and tourists eat there.

1. What is Aoi asking about?
   a. The hotel   **b.** The Marina Bay area   **c.** Food courts

▶▶▶▶ ◀◀◀◀ 🔊 Audio 2-06

Emily: We want to have high tea tomorrow. Where would you recommend we go?
Guide: I'd recommend either the Raffles Hotel or the Fullerton Hotel.
Emily: Which is closer to our hotel?
Guide: The Raffles. I think _____.

2. How will Aoi and Emily most likely get to the Raffles Hotel?
   a. By taxi   **b.** They will most likely walk there.   **c.** By bus

▶▶▶▶ ◀◀◀◀ 🔊 Audio 2-07

Emily: We can go to Newton Circus by MRT, right?
Guide: That's right. You can take one at City Hall and get off at Newton. _____.
Emily: OK. Is it easy to find the station?

▶MRT：地下鉄

3. How many stops is Newton from City Hall?
   a. Two   **b.** Three   **c.** Four

ツアーガイドとの会話―観光

Unit 10 Singapore: High Tea at the Raffles Hotel, Anyone?

日常会話＋ｅメールで—観光

アオイとエミリーはガーデンズ・バイ・ザ・ベイとマリーナベイ・サンズ・ホテルに行く。その後、ラッフルズ・ホテルに行きハイティーをする。夕方、チャイナタウンでしばらく散策した後、ニュートン・サーカスに行き夕食。明日はいよいよオーストラリア。エミリーの実家があるパースへ行く。

Words & Phrases
次の１〜10の語または語句の最も適切な意味を下のａ〜ｊから選びなさい。

1. observation deck
2. As I recall
3. author
4. be comprised of
5. luxury hotel
6. roof
7. definitely
8. a bit of
9. crab
10. nocturnal animal

a. カニ
b. 絶対に
c. 高級ホテル
d. （ビルの）屋上
e. 展望台
f. 著者
g. 夜行性動物
h. ・・・から成る
i. 少しの
j. 私の記憶するところでは

Warm-up
音声を聴いて、１〜３のダイアログの空所を埋めましょう。　　　Audio 2-08

At breakfast

1. **Emily:** Did you sleep ¹_____ last night?
   Aoi: Yes, I did. I wanted to sleep ²_____, though.
   Emily: Me, too. I wish we had thirty hours in a day.

2. **Aoi:** Are we going to the Marina Bay Sands Hotel this morning?
   Emily: Yes. We'll be going up to the ³_____ deck.
   Aoi: I want to take a look at the ⁴_____, too.

3. **Emily:** I'm hanging out for high tea at the Raffles Hotel.
   Aoi: So am I. It's ⁵_____ to be one of the best here.
   Emily: As I ⁶_____, Somerset Maugham, author of *The Moon and Sixpence* once stayed at the Raffles.

Exercise 1

1〜7の（ ）内の語または語句を並べかえて英文を完成させましょう。ただし、文頭にくるものも小文字で与えています。次に音声を聴いて答を確認しましょう。

🔊 Audio 2-09

1. シンガポールでは車を購入する際、まず車両購入権 (COE) を取得しなければなりません。
   You must first (a COE, a new car, register, obtain, to) in Singapore.
   _____

2. 多くの若いシンガポール人は2か国語以上話すことができます。
   (able, two, Singaporeans, young, are, speak, to, many, or more languages).
   _____

3. ブキテイト・ティマ・ヒルは標高163メートルで最も高いところです。
   Bukit Timah Hill, (above, at, level, 163m, sea), is the highest natural point.
   _____

4. シンガポール航空は世界で高い評価を受けています。
   Singapore Airlines (reputation, world, earned, a, the, has, great, throughout).
   _____

5. 神話上のマーライオンはライオンの頭部と魚の体を持っています。
   The mythical Merlion (a fish, of, has, and the body, a lion's head).
   _____

6. シンガポールの初代の首相が誰か知っていますか？
   (of Singapore, you, who, the, do, prime minister, know, first, was)?
   _____

7. 多くのシンガポール人は多忙なライフスタイルのため大抵フードコートで食事をすませます。
   Many Singaporeans (food courts, busy, due to, often eat, at, lifestyles, their, out).
   _____

Exercise 2

1〜4の英文の音声を聴いて、(*) に入る語をa〜cから選び、記号で答えなさい。

🔊 Audio 2-10

1. There is a (　) (　) (*) (　) (　).
   a. on b. the c. pool

2. The Raffles (　) (　) (*) (　) (　).
   a. luxury b. a c. colonial-style

3. (　) (　) (*) (　) (　) MRT.
   a. to b. go c. Chinatown

4. (　) (　) (*) (　) (　).
   a. for b. we're c. leaving

日常会話＋eメールで観光

Exercise 3 次の電子メールを読んで以下の質問に答えましょう。

Dear Judy,

Emily and I are in Singapore now. We have just visited the Marina Bay Sands Hotel and Gardens by the Bay. The Marina Bay Sands Hotel is comprised of three 57-story towers. There is a swimming pool on the roof, which is only [1](   ) (   ) (   ) staying at the hotel. Gardens by the Bay is a [2](   ) (   ) (   ).

High tea at the Tiffin Room in the Raffles Hotel was wonderful. The Raffles is a colonial-style luxury hotel and is definitely [3](   ) (   ) (   ).

This evening we're going to Chinatown by MRT. Then we're going to Newton Circus for dinner. You can enjoy a variety of [4](   ) (   ) (   ) there.

Tomorrow we're leaving for Australia. We'll visit Perth first, then Sydney and Cairns. We'll be staying at Emily's house in Perth. So many unique animals I've never seen … I can hardly wait.

I'll write again soon.

Your friend,
Aoi

Q1 音声を聴いて、Email の空所 1 〜 4 を埋めましょう。　　Audio 2-11

Q2 Email の内容について、音声を聴き最も適切な答を a 〜 c の中から選びましょう。

Audio 2-11

1. How many towers is the Marina Bay Sands Hotel comprised of?
    a. Two   **b.** Three   **c.** Four
2. Where will Aoi and Emily have dinner?
    a. In Chinatown   **b.** At the Raffles Hotel   **c.** At Newton Circus
3. Which city in Australia does Emily's family live in?
    a. Sydney   **b.** Cairns   **c.** Perth

📍 Challenge Corner

ダイアログの音声を聴いて、░░の部分を書き取り、1～3の質問に対して最も適切な答をa～cの中から選びましょう。

▶▶▶▶ ◀◀◀◀　　🔊 Audio 2-12

Emily: How about going to Clarke Quay first, since we still have a bit of time?
Aoi: What do you want to do there?
Emily: Well, _____. The best view of the Marina Bay area can be enjoyed from the river.

1. How long is the cruise?
　　a. Half an hour　　b. 40 minutes　　c. 50 minutes

At Newton Circus

▶▶▶▶ ◀◀◀◀　　🔊 Audio 2-13

Emily: Let's look around to see which stalls seem to serve the best food.
Aoi: OK. What do you feel like eating tonight?
Emily: We had chilli crab last night, so _____.

2. What will Aoi and Emily most likely eat tonight?
　　a. Chilli crab
　　b. Black pepper crab
　　c. Both chilli crab and black pepper crab

Back in the hotel room

▶▶▶▶ ◀◀◀◀　　🔊 Audio 2-14

Aoi: Next time I'm here, I want to go to the Night Safari.
Emily: If you like nocturnal animals, you'll like that zoo.
Aoi: Have you been there before?
Emily: Yes, I've been once. _____ the first time we came to Singapore.

3. Who did Emily go to the Night Safari with?
　　a. Her parents　　b. Her sister　　c. Both her parents and her sister

Unit 11 Perth: Emily's Family Meets Aoi

到着後の空港では

アオイとエミリーはエミリーの生まれ育ったパースへ向けシンガポールを出発。なんと言ってもオーストラリアへの旅行は今回が初めてだし、本格的なホームステイだって未経験。入国手続きの前に免税店でお土産を買う。さて、ようやく到着ロビーでエミリーの両親と初顔合わせ。

Words & Phrases

次の1〜10の語または語句の最も適切な意味を下のa〜jから選びなさい。

1. land
2. duty-free shop
3. a little bit
4. worry
5. pleasure
6. get changed
7. Here we are.
8. Home sweet home
9. shy
10. a quick tour of the house

a. 喜び
b. 着替える
c. ほんの少し
d. あ〜、我が家だ
e. さあ着いた。
f. 心配する
g. 免税店
h. 家の中の簡単な案内
i. 着陸する
j. 恥ずかしそうな

Warm-up

音声を聴いて、1〜3のダイアログの空所を埋めましょう。

Audio 2-15

After landing at Perth Airport

1. **Emily:** Have you ^{1}_____ everything?
   Aoi: Yeah, I think so.
   Emily: OK, ^{2}_____. Let's go.

2. **Emily:** Just let me stop at the duty-free shop before we go ^{3}_____ immigration.
   Aoi: Can you do that?
   Emily: Sure. I just want to get something for my ^{4}_____.

3. **Emily:** Are you ^{5}_____?
   Aoi: Yes. A little bit.
   Emily: Don't worry. My parents are coming to ^{6}_____ us ^{7}____.

Exercise 1
1〜7の（　）内の語または語句を並べかえて英文を完成させましょう。ただし、文頭にくるものも小文字で与えています。次に音声を聴いて答を確認しましょう。

🔊 Audio 2-16

1. 現在の天気は晴れで気温は摂氏17度です。
   (and, clear, current, is, the, weather) 17°C.
   _____

2. 空港の建物内の喫煙は固く禁じられています。
   Smoking (airport, inside, is, prohibited, strictly, the) building.
   _____

3. すべての持ち物を入国カードに申告する必要があります。
   You (all, declare, items, must, on, your) Incoming Passenger Card.
   _____

4. 公的な場所では荷物を決して放置してはいけません。
   Baggage (be, in, left, must, never, unattended) public areas.
   _____

5. 手荷物受取は入国審査の後となっています。
   You (after, baggage, collect, immigration, your, can).
   _____

6. パース空港には4つのターミナルがあります。
   (are, at, four, Perth Airport, terminals, there).
   _____

7. 空港は都心から約10キロの東に位置しています。
   (airport, is, east, of, the, about, the city centre, located, 10km).
   _____

Exercise 2
1〜4の英文の音声を聴いて、（　＊　）に入る語をa〜cから選び、記号で答えなさい。

🔊 Audio 2-17

1. Did (　) (　) (＊) (　) (　)?
   a. a   **b.** good   **c.** have

2. Oh, (　) (　) (＊) (　) (　).
   a. waiting   **b.** the   **c.** in

3. It's (　) (　) (＊) (　) (　), Ms. Atkins.
   a. pleasure   **b.** meet   **c.** to

4. Do you need to do anything (　) (　) (＊) (　) (　) car?
   a. go   **b.** we   **c.** to

到着後の空港では

Exercise 3

音声を聴いて、ダイアログの空所 1 〜 4 を埋めましょう。次に 1 〜 3 の質問に対する答として最も適切なものを a 〜 c の中から選びましょう。

🔊 Audio 2-18

In the arrivals lobby

Ms. Atkins: Welcome home, Emily.
お帰り、エミリー。

Emily: Hi, Mum. Great to see you again. ¹(   ) (   ) (   ) (   )?
ただいま、お母さん。また会えてうれしいわ。元気?

Ms. Atkins: Not bad. Did you have a good flight?
まあまあよ。空の旅は快適だった?

Emily: Yes, we did. Where's Dad?
うん、良かったよ。お父さんはどこ?

Ms. Atkins: Oh, he's waiting in the car. Hello. ²(   ) (   ) (   ) Aoi.
車の中で待っているわ。こんにちは。あなたがアオイね。

Aoi: Yes, I am. It's a pleasure to meet you, Ms. Atkins.
はい、そうです。お目にかかれて光栄です、アトキンス夫人。

Ms. Atkins: It's nice to meet you, too. ³(   ) (   ) (   ) Joan.
こちらこそ初めまして。どうぞジョーンと呼んでね。

Aoi: OK, Joan.
はい、ジョーンさん。

Ms. Atkins: Do you need to do anything before we go to the car?
車に行く前に何かしなきゃいけないことある?

Aoi: I'd like to ⁴(   ) (   ) (   ), if I can.
できればちょっと両替したいのですが。

1. Who is in the arrivals lobby to meet Emily and Aoi?
   a. Mr. Atkins   b. Ms. Atkins   c. Mr. and Ms. Atkins
2. How was the flight?
   a. It was a pleasure.   b. It was bad.   c. It was good.
3. What does Aoi want to do before going to the car?
   a. Change some money   b. Get changed   c. Meet Emily's dad

📍 Challenge Corner

ダイアログの音声を聴いて、▭の部分を書き取り、1～3の質問に対して最も適切な答をa～cの中から選びましょう。

▶▶▶▶ ◀◀◀◀   📶 Audio 2-19

Mr. Atkins: Hello, how are you?
Emily: Good. Dad, this is Aoi. Aoi, this is my dad. _____.
Aoi: Hello, Bob. Thank you for coming to pick us up.

1. What does Aoi call Emily's father?
 a. Bob   **b.** Dad   **c.** Mr. Atkins

After arriving at the Atkins' house

▶▶▶▶ ◀◀◀◀   📶 Audio 2-20

Emily: Here we are. Home sweet home.
Mr. Atkins: You ladies can go inside. _____.
Emily: OK. Thanks, Dad.

2. Who is going to carry the luggage inside the house?
 a. Aoi   **b.** Emily   **c.** Mr. Atkins

▶▶▶▶ ◀◀◀◀   📶 Audio 2-21

Emily: Don't be shy. Come in!
Aoi: Thank you. What a beautiful home!
Emily: Let me give you a quick tour of the house. OK. _____.
Here's the toilet. And here's the bathroom. Let me know if you need anything.

3. Which room does Emily show Aoi first?
 a. The bathroom   **b.** Aoi's room   **c.** The toilet

Unit 12 Perth: Where City Meets Outback

友だちの家族宅に泊まる─観光

早朝、外からの不思議なモーニングコールで目覚めたアオイ。その正体はアトキンス家の庭に暮らしているワライカワセミだったことが判明。アオイは野生動物に会いに行きたい。もちろん、エミリーの通っていた大学や街の中心部、その真向かいにあるキングス・パークやスワン川も見物する予定。

Words & Phrases

次の 1 ～ 10 の語または語句の最も適切な意味を下の a ～ j から選びなさい。

1. cackling sound
2. kookaburra
3. alarm clock
4. wild
5. on one's way to
6. if you like
7. first of all
8. kid
9. drop in
10. on one's way back

a. からかう
b. まず第一に
c. ワライカワセミ
d. ひょいと立ち寄る
e. 目覚し時計
f. 野生の
g. 帰りがけに
h. クワックワッという音
i. もしよければ
j. …に行く途中で

Warm-up

音声を聴いて、1 ～ 3 のダイアログの空所を埋めましょう。　　Audio 2-22

In the living room

1. **Ms. Atkins:** Good morning, Aoi. Did you sleep well?
   Aoi: I did. But I was woken up by a ¹_____ cackling sound outside.
   Ms. Atkins: That would have been a ²_____ kookaburra. They're also known as the 'bushman's alarm clock.'
2. **Aoi:** Will I be able to see any wild koalas while I'm in Perth?
   Ms. Atkins: Not wild koalas, but you can see some at the ³_____.
   Aoi: Really? That would be ⁴_____.
3. **Mr. Atkins:** So, ladies, what are your plans for the day?
   Emily: Well, we are going to see the black ⁵_____ at Lake Monger, then the city and King's Park.
   Mr. Atkins: I can ⁶_____ you off on my way to work, if you like.

■ Exercise 1　1〜7の（　）内の語または語句を並べかえて英文を完成させましょう。ただし、文頭にくるものも小文字で与えています。次に音声を聴いて答を確認しましょう。

🔊 Audio 2-23

1. パースには市内バスが無料の地域があります。
   (a, city buses, Perth, for, Free Transit Zone, has).
   _____

2. 乗車券は２時間有効となっています。
   (for, your, hours, is, two, ticket, valid).
   _____

3. ペンギン島はパースから４５分ほどの南に位置しています。
   Penguin Island (of, 45 minutes, located, Perth, is, south, about).
   _____

4. キングズ・パークは世界の都心部にある公園の中で一番大きな公園の一つです。
   King's Park is (in, of, inner-city, largest, one, parks, the) the world.
   _____

5. 自転車を列車内に持ち込むのは、混雑していない時間帯ならば可能です。
   Bicycles (peak, OK, on trains, outside, are, travel times).
   _____

6. 西オーストラリア州では公共の場での飲酒は違法です。
   In Western Australia, it (an, drink, in, offence, public, to, is).
   _____

7. ロットネスト島原産の哺乳類はクアッカワラビーだけです。
   The quokka (mammal, is, native, only, to, the) Rottnest Island.
   _____

■ Exercise 2　1〜4の英文の音声を聴いて、（　＊　）に入る語をa〜cから選び、記号で答えなさい。

🔊 Audio 2-24

1. It's about a ten-minute (　　) (　　) (　＊　) (　　) (　　).
   a. the　　b. from　　c. ride

2. (　　) (　　) (　＊　) (　　) (　　), if we have time.
   a. later　　b. you　　c. there

3. (　　) (　　) (　＊　) (　　) (　　) The Tavern.
   a. even　　b. go　　c. could

4. (　　) (　　) (　＊　) (　　) (　　) Perth Mint.
   a. you　　b. to　　c. take

友だちの家族宅に泊まる―観光

Exercise 3 音声を聴いて、ダイアログの空所 1 ～ 4 を埋めましょう。次に 1 ～ 3 の質問に対する答として最も適切なものを a ～ c の中から選びましょう。

🔊 Audio 2-25

Just before leaving the house

Aoi: So tell me, Emily, where did you go to university?
ねえ、エミリーってどこの大学に通ったの？

Emily: I went to the University of Western Australia. It's about a ten-minute bus ride from the city. I'll take you there later, if we have time.
西オーストラリア大学に行ってたわ。パースの市内からバスで 10 分ぐらい。時間があれば後で連れて行ってあげるよ。

Aoi: Great! I'd like that.
すごい！　ぜひお願いね。

Emily: We could even go to The Tavern and I could introduce you to some of our ¹(   ) (   ) (   ).
キャンパスのパブに行ったら、おいしい地ビールだって飲めるよ。

Aoi: You've got to be kidding. There's a ²(   ) (   ) (   )?
冗談でしょう！　キャンパスにパブがあるなんて？

Emily: You bet there is. Anyway, we're going to Lake Monger first. Then I'll take you to the Perth Mint and King's Park.
それがあるのよ。とりあえず、最初にモンガー湖に行って、その後パース造幣局とキングス・パークに連れて行くわ。

Aoi: Sounds exciting. Does the Mint have a ³(   ) (   ), too?
面白そうね。その造幣局にはお土産屋さんもあるのかしら。

Emily: It does. You can buy ⁴(   ) (   ) (   ) (   ), gifts and jewellery.
あるわ。ありとあらゆる硬貨、土産物それに宝石が買えるわ。

1. Why is Aoi surprised?
   a. Emily must be kidding.
   b. You can bet on campus.
   c. There is a university tavern.

2. Where are Aoi and Emily going first of all?
   a. To the university   b. To the Perth Mint   c. To Lake Monger

3. What can you buy at the Perth Mint?
   a. Beer   b. Gifts   c. Peppermint

Challenge Corner

ダイアログの音声を聴いて、　　の部分を書き取り、1〜3の質問に対して最も適切な答をa〜cの中から選びましょう。

Back at Emily's house

▶▶▶▶ ◀◀◀◀　　　　　　　　　Audio 2-26

Ms. Atkins: Emily, _____?
Emily: Of course. What would you like us to do?
Ms. Atkins: Can you set the table outside and make some potato salad?

1. What does Ms. Atkins want?
   a. A table　　　b. Two hands　　　c. Some help

▶▶▶▶ ◀◀◀◀　　　　　　　　　Audio 2-27

Aoi: What are you having?
Emily: A flat white.
Aoi: What's that?
Emily: As Hugh Jackman said, it's 'like a latte _____.'

2. What's in a flat white?
   a. Milk　　　b. Espresso　　　c. Both milk and espresso

▶▶▶▶ ◀◀◀◀　　　　　　　　　Audio 2-28

Mr. Atkins: Why don't we take Aoi to Penguin Island tomorrow?
Ms. Atkins: And _____ the Fremantle Markets on our way back, too.
Mr. Atkins: Now that's a good idea.

3. How many places are mentioned in the dialogue?
   a. One　　　b. Two　　　c. Three

友だちの家族宅に泊まる — 観光

Unit 13 Sydney: The Harbour City

日常会話―観光

エミリーの両親との別れを惜しみながら、アオイとエミリーは東海岸の大都会シドニーへ出発。ホテルにチェックイン後は市内観光へ繰り出す。アオイはハーバーブリッジに心惹かれ、オージービーフやパンケーキに舌鼓を打つ。さらなる楽しみはパースでついぞお目にかかれなかった野生のコアラだ。

Words & Phrases

次の1〜10の語または語句の最も適切な意味を下のa〜jから選びなさい。

1. hostel
2. next to
3. how often
4. clothing
5. host
6. feel like
7. in business
8. main course
9. grill
10. mash

a. メインの料理
b. （会などを）主催する
c. 簡易宿泊所
d. ・・・の隣に
e. （飲食物等）が欲しい
f. ・・・をすりつぶす
g. 衣料品
h. どのくらいの頻度で
i. （会社等が）業務を続けている
j. （肉などを）網焼きにする

Warm-up

音声を聴いて、1〜3のダイアログの空所を埋めましょう。 Audio 2-29

After landing at Sydney Airport

1. **Emily:** That was a long flight, wasn't it?
   Aoi: You're not ¹_____ . It took more than four hours.
   Emily: It ²_____ you how big this country is.
2. **Aoi:** How are we getting from here to our ³_____ hostel?
   Emily: We're taking the train. It takes just ⁴_____ minutes to the city. The hostel is right next to Central Station.
   Aoi: How often do the trains run?
3. **Aoi:** What are those people in the ⁵_____ doing, Emily?
   Emily: They're playing cricket. It's often called Australia's ⁶_____ sport.
   Aoi: I've never seen it before. How do you play it?

Exercise 1
1～7の（　）内の語または語句を並べかえて英文を完成させましょう。ただし、文頭にくるものも小文字で与えています。次に音声を聴いて答を確認しましょう。

🔊 Audio 2-30

1. エアポートリンクという電車を利用する際は、オパールカードを購入しなければなりません。
To use the Airport Link train service, (to, an, need, Opal Card, purchase, you).
_____

2. シドニーはパースより2時間進んでいます。
(ahead, hours, is, Perth, of, Sydney, two).
_____

3. シドニーハーバーブリッジは1932年3月に正式にオープンしました。
(in, was, March 1932, officially, the, opened, Sydney Harbour Bridge).
_____

4. ラグビーリーグはシドニーで最も人気のあるスポーツです。
The (in, is, sport, most, rugby league, the, popular) Sydney.
_____

5. 世界最悪のクモをシドニーで見つけることができます。
The world's (can, deadliest, found, spider, be) in Sydney.
_____

6. 国内空港はセントラル駅からわずか6つ目の駅です。
The (airport, six, Central Station, domestic, from, is, only, stops).
_____

7. ボンダイビーチはオーストラリアで最も多くの観光客が訪れる場所の一つです。
Bondi Beach (is, most, of, one, sites, the, tourist, visited) in Australia.
_____

Exercise 2
1～4の英文の音声を聴いて、（ * ）に入る語をa～cから選び、記号で答えなさい。

🔊 Audio 2-31

1. (　) (　) (*) (　) (　) for us?
 a. got　　b. you　　c. have

2. Once (　) (　) (*) (　) (　),
 a. into　　b. checked　　c. our

3. I know (　) (　) (*) (　) (　).
 a. sweet　　b. a　　c. got

4. We might be able to catch (　) (　) (*) (　) (　).
 a. some　　b. of　　c. glimpse

日常会話―観光

Exercise 3　音声を聴いて、ダイアログの空所1～4を埋めましょう。次に1～3の質問に対する答として最も適切なものをa～cの中から選びましょう。

🔊 Audio 2-32

On the train to the city

Aoi: So, Emily, what have you got planned for us while we're in Sydney?
ねえエミリー、シドニーに滞在中どんな計画を立てているの？

Emily: Well, once we've checked into our hostel, I thought I could ¹(　　) (　　) (　　) to see the Opera House and the 'Coathanger.'
そうね、ホステルにチェックインした後に、オペラハウスや「コートハンガー」に案内しようと思ってるの。

Aoi: The 'Coathanger?' What's that?
「コートハンガー」？　何それ？

Emily: That's what the locals affectionately call the Sydney Harbour Bridge. They also have a bridge climb, if you're interested.
シドニーハーバーブリッジのことを地元の人は親しみを込めてそう呼ぶの。もし興味があれば、橋に上ることもできるわよ。

Aoi: I think I'll ²(　　) (　　) (　　) (　　).
橋に上るのは止めとくわ。

Emily: I know you've got a sweet tooth, so I'll take you to this ³(　　) (　　) (　　) in the Rocks near the Harbour Bridge.
あなたは甘党だから、ハーバーブリッジ近くのロックスにあるこの有名なパンケーキ屋さんに連れて行ってあげる。

Aoi: And what about tomorrow?
じゃあ、明日はどうする？

Emily: Well, ⁴(　　) (　　) (　　) on a full-day tour to the Blue Mountains. We might be able to catch a glimpse of some koalas in the wild there.
うん、ブルーマウンテンへの丸一日のツアーを予約してるわ。もしかしたら、そこでちらっと野生のコアラを見ることができるかもしれないわよ。

1. What is the 'Coathanger'?
   a. A bridge　　b. A clothing store　　c. A pancake restaurant

2. Does Aoi like sweet food?
   a. No, she doesn't.　　b. Yes, she does.　　c. It's not mentioned.

3. What might Aoi and Emily be able to see tomorrow?
   a. Pancakes　　b. Koalas　　c. Rocks

📍 Challenge Corner

ダイアログの音声を聴いて、░░░の部分を書き取り、1〜3の質問に対して最も適切な答をa〜cの中から選びましょう。

▶▶▶▶ ◀◀◀◀   🔊 Audio 2-33

Aoi: What's in Homebush, Emily?

Emily: _____. They used it to host for Sydney 2000.

Aoi: I remember now. That's when Naoko Takahashi won gold in the women's marathon, right?

1. What is in Homebush?
   a. Emily's home
   b. Naoko Takahashi's home
   c. The Olympic Stadium

▶▶▶▶ ◀◀◀◀   🔊 Audio 2-34

Emily: What do you feel like for lunch today?

Aoi: You know, _____ fish 'n' chips.

Emily: Oh, that's easy. We can take a ferry from Circular Quay to Watson's Bay. There's a seafood restaurant there that's been in business since 1885.

2. Has Aoi ever eaten fish 'n' chips?
   a. No, never.   b. Yes, many times.   c. Yes, once.

▶▶▶▶ ◀◀◀◀   🔊 Audio 2-35

Waiter: Hello. Are you ready to order?

Aoi: What do you recommend?

Waiter: The Surf and Turf is very good. _____ combining a 250g fillet steak and grilled bugs with mashed potato.

3. What is Surf and Turf?
   a. It's a dessert.   b. It's a dish.   c. It's a drink.

日常会話―観光

Unit 14 Cairns: Gateway to the Reef

到着後の空港では／タクシーに乗ったら

ケアンズはオーストラリアのグレート・バリア・リーフの玄関。この春休みの長い冒険の最後の舞台。ケアンズは都会というより田舎町に近い。思いっきりケアンズの自然と一体化しよう。最終日、荷造りをしながら大学の友人たちへのお土産をまだ買っていないことに気がつく。

Words & Phrases 次の1～10の語または語句の最も適切な意味を下のa～jから選びなさい。

1. taxi stand
2. There you go.
3. change
4. tourist attraction
5. concierge
6. fun-filled
7. come in
8. sunscreen
9. goodies
10. brochure

   a. パンフレット
   b. 楽しさいっぱいの
   c. おいしい物
   d. 日焼け止めクリーム
   e. 観光名所
   f. タクシー乗り場
   g. おつり
   h. (ホテルなどの) 接客係
   i. さあどうぞ。
   j. …の色／サイズで売られる

Warm-up 音声を聴いて、1～3のダイアログの空所を埋めましょう。

 Audio 2-36

After landing at Cairns Airport

1. **Aoi:** Excuse me. Where is the taxi stand?
   Clerk: The taxi stand is right ¹_____ the airport terminal. Go out through those doors and ²_____ left.
   Aoi: Thank you very much.

2. **Driver:** Good afternoon. ³_____ are you going?
   Emily: The Coral Tree Inn.
   Driver: ⁴_____.

3. **Driver:** Here we are. The Coral Tree Inn. ⁵_____ $22.50.
   Emily: Thanks. There you go.
   Driver: Out of $25. That's $2.50 change. Enjoy your ⁶_____.

Exercise 1

1～7の（　）内の語または語句を並べかえて英文を完成させましょう。ただし、文頭にくるものも小文字で与えています。次に音声を聴いて答を確認しましょう。

🔊 Audio 2-37

1. ケアンズ・ラグーンはケアンズの街の浜辺にある大型のリゾートタイプのプールです。
The Cairns Lagoon (a, giant, is, on, pool, resort-style, swimming, the) city's foreshore.
_____

2. 雨季はさらにワニに注意すべき時期です。
The wet season (a, be, extra, is, time, to, wary) of crocodiles.
_____

3. デインツリーは世界中で最も古い熱帯雨林です。
The Daintree (in, is, oldest, rainforest, the, tropical) the world.
_____

4. ケアンズはオーストラリアのグレート・バリア・リーフの玄関と考えられています。
(Australia's, Cairns, considered, gateway, is, the, to) Great Barrier Reef.
_____

5. グレート・バリア・リーフは世界の七つの自然の驚異の一つです。
The Great Barrier Reef (is, Natural, of, one, Seven, the, Wonders) of the World.
_____

6. モンスーンの大雨がある雨季は11月から5月までです。
The wet season (and, downpours, runs, monsoonal, has, heavy) from November to May.
_____

7. レストランでは、B.Y.O. は酒類を持ち込むことができることを表しています。
In a restaurant, (alcohol, bring, B.Y.O., for, own, stands, your).
_____

Exercise 2

1～4の英文の音声を聴いて、（ ＊ ）に入る語をa～cから選び、記号で答えなさい。

🔊 Audio 2-38

1. (　　) (　　) (＊) (　　) (　　)?
　a. I　　　b. help　　　c. may

2. (　　) (　　) (＊) (　　) (　　).
　a. check　　b. like　　c. to

3. A (　　) (　　) (＊) (　　) (　　)?
　a. three　　b. for　　c. room

4. (　　) (　　) (＊) (　　) (　　) an impression of your credit card.
　a. to　　　b. need　　c. just

Exercise 3 音声を聴いて、ダイアログの空所 1 〜 4 を埋めましょう。次に 1 〜 3 の質問に対する答として最も適切なものを a 〜 c の中から選びましょう。

🔊 Audio 2-39

At the hotel

Front desk: Good afternoon. How may I help you?
こんにちは。いらっしゃいませ。

Emily: We'd like to check in.
チェックインしたいのですが。

Front desk: Of course. Do you [1](　　　) (　　　) (　　　)?
かしこまりました。ご予約はされていますか？

Emily: Yes, we do.
はい。

Front desk: [2](　　　) (　　　), (　　　)?
お名前をお伺いしてもよろしいですか？

Emily: Emily Atkins and Aoi Manabe.
エミリー・アトキンスとアオイ・マナベです。

Front desk: One moment, please. Ah, yes. [3](　　　) (　　　) (　　　). Ms Emily Atkins and Ms Aoi Manabe. A twin room for three nights?
少々お待ちください。はい、こちらにございます。エミリー・アトキンス様とアオイ・マナベ様ですね。ツインルームで 3 泊ですね？

Emily: That's right.
ええ、そうです。

Front desk: I'll just need to take an impression of your credit card and ask you to fill out this [4](　　　) (　　　) (　　　).
お客様のクレジットカードを読み取り機に通させていただきます。それから、こちらの顧客登録カードにご記入をお願いいたします。

Emily: Here you are.
はい、どうぞ。

1. How long are Aoi and Emily staying?
   a. One night　　b. Two nights　　c. Three nights
2. Did the front desk clerk ask Emily for her credit card?
   a. Yes, he did.　　b. No, he didn't.　　c. Yes, it did.
3. What time of day is it?
   a. Morning　　b. Afternoon　　c. Evening

Challenge Corner

ダイアログの音声を聴いて、　の部分を書き取り、1～3の質問に対して最も適切な答をa～cの中から選びましょう。

🔊 Audio 2-40

Concierge: Good afternoon. Can I help you?
Emily: We'd like to find out about things to do in Cairns.
Concierge: Sure. _____ have information about activities and tourist attractions for a fun-filled holiday.

1. Did the concierge give Aoi and Emily something to look at?
   a. Yes, he did.   b. No, he didn't.   c. We don't know.

🔊 Audio 2-41

Emily: Excuse me. How much are these T-shirts?
Shop clerk: They're $ 15 each.
Emily: What sizes do you have?
Shop clerk: We have _____. And they come in blue, green, red, black and orange.

2. How many different sizes do the T-shirts come in?
   a. Three   b. Four   c. Five

🔊 Audio 2-42

Aoi: Is the supermarket still open?
Emily: I think so. What do you need?
Aoi: I want to pick up some sunscreen _____.
Emily: That's a good idea. Let's pick up some goodies to take with us, too.

3. Where are Aoi and Emily going tomorrow?
   a. Diving   b. To a souvenir shop   c. To a supermarket

Unit 15 Back in Japan
日常会話＋SNS で

アオイとエミリーは無事日本に戻る。アオイは４月から４年生となり就職活動を始める。英語を使って働ける仕事に就きたい。彼女はゼミで今回の旅行について英語で発表するので、書き上げた原稿をエミリーにチェックしてもらう。

Words & Phrases
次の１～10の語または語句の最も適切な意味を下のa～jから選びなさい。

1. say hello to
2. deliver
3. text message
4. cousin
5. at first
6. worse
7. have in mind
8. be assigned to
9. prefer
10. abroad

a. いとこ
b. ・・・を好む
c. 海外に
d. ・・・を考慮している
e. より悪い
f. 携帯電話で送るメッセージ
g. 最初（のうち）は
h. ・・・に任じられる
i. （論文など）を口頭発表する
j. ・・・によろしくと伝える

Warm-up
音声を聴いて、１～３のダイアログの空所を埋めましょう。 Audio 2-43

1. **Emily:** Have you seen John here on campus [1]_____?
   Aoi: No, I haven't. I don't think he's back from Chicago yet.
   Emily: I [2]_____ he'd be back by now.

2. **Emily:** I talked with my parents on LINE last night.
   Aoi: How are they getting [3]_____?
   Emily: They're doing fine. They told me to say [4]_____ to you.

3. **Aoi:** I'm making a presentation about our [5]_____ in my English class.
   Emily: Good idea. Are you going to [6]_____ it in English?
   Aoi: I am. Please proofread my draft once I've finished writing it.

Exercise 1

1〜7の（　）内の語または語句を並べかえて英文を完成させましょう。ただし、文頭にくるものも小文字で与えています。次に音声を聴いて答を確認しましょう。

🔊 Audio 2-44

1. 彼の到着予定は午後3時15分です。
He (a, arrive, at, to, is, quarter, scheduled) past three p.m.

_____

2. ハナは春休みの間フィリピンでボランティア活動をしました。
Hana (during, work, in the Philippines, volunteer, did) the spring holidays.

_____

3. 私は世界中を旅して様々な文化に触れたいです。
I want to (different cultures, the world, experience, many, travel, to).

_____

4. 彼は後期のすべてのテストに合格しました。
He (second, of his, in, passed, all, semester, tests).

_____

5. 新学期はあと2週間で始まります。
(another, semester, weeks, starts, the, two, in, new).

_____

6. 彼女は皆の前で英語で発表しなければいけません。
She (everyone, front, give, to, in, a presentation, has, of).

_____

7. 大学の4年生は就職活動に真剣に取り組んでいます。
(about, fourth-year, serious, the, job hunting, are, students, university).

_____

Exercise 2

1〜4の英文の音声を聴いて、（ * ）に入る語をa〜cから選び、記号で答えなさい。

🔊 Audio 2-45

1. (　　) (　　) (*) (　　) (　　) leaving for Australia.
　a. supposed　　**b.** be　　**c.** to

2. She took me to places (　　) (　　) (*) (　　) (　　) go.
　a. not　　**b.** do　　**c.** tourists

3. (　　) (　　) (*) (　　) (　　) it.
　a. of　　**b.** every　　**c.** minute

4. (　　) (　　) (*) (　　) (　　) starts,
　a. academic　　**b.** new　　**c.** year

日常会話＋SNSで

Exercise 3 音声を聴いて、ダイアログの空所 1 〜 4 を埋めましょう。次に 1 〜 3 の質問に対する答として最も適切なものを a 〜 c の中から選びましょう。

🔊 Audio 2-46

Talking on LINE

Judy
How was Australia? When I ¹( ) ( ) ( ) ( ) from Singapore, you were supposed to be leaving for Australia the next day.
オーストラリアはどうだった？ シンガポールからあなたの最後のメールを受け取った時、あなたはその翌日オーストラリアに行くことになっていたわ。

Aoi
That's right. The following day we flew to Perth and stayed at Emily's there for a week. She took me to places where tourists do not usually go.
そう。翌日パースまで飛んで、そこではエミリーの自宅に 1 週間滞在したのよ。彼女は旅行者が普通は行かないようなところに案内してくれたわ。

Judy
Sounds interesting. So you enjoyed every minute of it.
面白そうね。だったら存分に楽しんだんだ。

Aoi
I sure did. And ²( ) ( ) ( ) ( ) that I enjoyed Sydney and Cairns, too.
もちろん。それと言うまでもないけど、シドニーとケアンズも楽しかった。

Judy
Did you climb the Sydney Harbor Bridge?
シドニーのハーバーブリッジには上った？

Aoi
Did I climb it? Of course I did!
上ったですって？ もちろんよ！

Judy
I'd ³( ) ( ) ( ) ( ). I'm scared of heights.
私だったら絶対上ってないわ。高所恐怖症だから。

Aoi
By the way, when the new academic year starts, I'm going to talk about this trip in my class. Emily's been ⁴( ) ( ) ( ) ( ).
ところで、新学期が始まったら授業で今回の旅行のことを発表するつもり。エミリーが手伝ってくれてるの。

1. How long did Aoi stay in Perth?
   a. For five days   **b.** For seven days   **c.** For ten days

2. How many places in Australia did Aoi visit?
   a. Three   **b.** Four   **c.** Five

3. Who's going to talk about their trip in class?
   a. Judy   **b.** Aoi   **c.** Emily

📍 Challenge Corner

ダイアログの音声を聴いて、　　の部分を書き取り、1〜3の質問に対して最も適切な答をa〜cの中から選びましょう。

New Orleans

▶▶▶▶ ◀◀◀◀　　　　　　　　　　　　　　　🔊 Audio 2-47

Aoi: I received a text message from John yesterday. He was in New Orleans.
Emily: Really? What was he doing there?
Aoi: _____ and that he'd be coming back the day after tomorrow.

1. Who was John visiting in New Orleans?
　a. His uncle　　　b. His brother　　　c. His cousin

▶▶▶▶ ◀◀◀◀　　　　　　　　　　　　　　　🔊 Audio 2-48

Emily: How did your presentation go?
Aoi: I was nervous at first, but I think _____.
Emily: Great! I knew you could do it.
Aoi: Well, but for your big help, I would never have been able to.

2. How did the presentation turn out?
　a. It turned out to be as good as Aoi had expected.
　b. It turned out to be better than Aoi had expected.
　c. It turned out to be worse than Aoi had expected.

▶▶▶▶ ◀◀◀◀　　　　　　　　　　　　　　　🔊 Audio 2-49

Emily: What kind of job do you have in mind?
Aoi: I'm hoping to get a job at a company where I can use English.
Emily: If you get the kind of job you're looking for, you may be assigned to work abroad.
Aoi: If so, _____.

3. If Aoi is assigned to work abroad, what country would she prefer to work?
　a. In Singapore
　b. In Australia
　c. Either in Singapore or Australia

First Time Traveling Abroad
はじめての英会話コミュニケーション：旅行編

2019年4月15日　初版第1刷発行
2024年3月25日　初版第3刷発行

著　者　行時 潔／今川京子／Antony J. Parker

発行者　森　信久

発行所　株式会社　松柏社
〒 102-0072　東京都千代田区飯田橋 1-6-1
TEL 03 (3230) 4813（代表）
FAX 03 (3230) 4857
http://www.shohakusha.com
e-mail: info@shohakusha.com

装丁　　小島トシノブ（NONdesign）
挿絵　　うえむらのぶこ

印刷・製本　日経印刷株式会社
略号 = 747

Copyright © 2019 by Kiyoshi Yukitoki, Kyoko Imagawa & Antony J. Parker
本書を無断で複写・複製することを禁じます。